Landmark Visitors Guide

St Lucia

Don Philpott

Don Philpott is a journalist, author and broadcaster who has spent the last thirty years exploring the world as a writer. Born in Hull, England, he worked for twenty years with the Press Association, the UK national news agency. He founded and co-edited Footloose, an outdoor activities magazine in the UK.

He now lives in Florida and is associate publisher of a newspaper and magazine house. He has written more than 50 books on travel, wine, food, diet and health issues and the media.

Dedication

To my beautiful American Rose

Acknowledgements

I am indebted to the following for their considerable help in researching and writing this guidebook. American Airlines, Lou Hammond and associates, Nancy J. Friedman Associ... Sandels, Jeannine and Nick at Ti Kaye and the St Lucia ... as Randolph and Bonni...

Published by
Landmark Publishing
Ashbourne Hall, Cokayne Ave, Ashbourne,
Derbyshire DE6 1EJ England

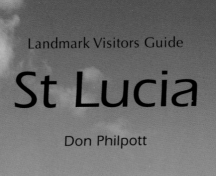

Landmark Visitors Guide

St Lucia

Don Philpott

Contents

FACTFILE

Feature Boxes

1. Before you go

Welcome to Paradise

Beautiful St Lucia (pronounced St Loo-sha) lies in the eastern Caribbean Sea about 21 miles (34km) south of Martinique and 26 miles (42km) north-east of St Vincent. Both can be seen on clear days. It is part of the West Indian archipelago which stretches for more than 2,000 miles (3,200km) from Cuba southwards to the northern coast of South America. It lies between 60° and 61° west longitude and 13° and 14° north latitude.

The island is the second largest of the Windward group, which themselves are part of the Lesser Antilles, and is 27 miles (43km) long and 14 miles (23km) wide, covering an area of 238sq miles (616sq.km), and with a population of around 140,000.

I LOVE ST.LUCIA

Castries, the sprawling capital and main port, is on the north-western coast, with a population of around 49,000 living in or around the city.

St Lucia has had a turbulent history and for centuries was fought over because of her strategic position. There were so many calls to arms that it earned the name **'Helen of the West Indies'**, which it still cherishes. The island changed hands 14 times as France and England vied for possession, it was the home of pirates and even saw a guillotine erected and used during the French Revolution. Today, there are few reminders of this troubled past, and the island is peaceful and beautiful. It has stunning, unspoilt palm tree-lined beaches, clear waters teeming with rainbow coloured fish, breathtaking scenery with its natural pyramids, drive-in volcano and tropical rain forests, and fabulous food. As you wander through the bustling fruit and vegetable market in Castries, vendors shout out "welcome to Paradise", and they could just be right.

GETTING TO ST LUCIA

BY AIR

The international airport is at Hewanorra just outside Vieux Fort, close to the southern tip of this island and about 40 miles (64km) from Castries and the main resort areas. Airlines using Hewanorra include British Airways, American Airlines, American Eagle, Air Jamaica, Amerijet International, Air Canada, BWIA, Helen Air and Virgin Atlantic.

There is the smaller George Charles airport at Vigie, just north of Castries, which has domestic and regional flights, and international flights from the USA on BWIA, LIAT, Eagle Air, American Eagle, Air Martinique and Helenair Caribbean.

From the UK — British Airways flies direct to St Lucia from London's Heathrow three times a week. Highest fares are in December and during the summer. Virgin Atlantic flies direct from Gatwick. Caledonian Airways has a weekly charter from Gatwick airport, and BWIA flies twice weekly. BWIA also serves other European destinations. There are also a number of charter flights between mid-November and mid-March.

From the USA — American Airlines flies between Orlando, Miami and New York's JFK International Airport to its Caribbean hub at San Juan on Puerto Rico, and then daily on to St Lucia's Hewanorra Airport. Highest fares are during the

Explorer Fares

Liat has a number of special passes, which are some of the best air deals anywhere and allow you to island-hop at bargain basement prices. There are the Explorer and and Super Explorer Fares which allow you to fly to several Caribbean islands on one trip at a flat fare, while the Liat Airpass allows visitors from Europe to fly to between three and six islands at a rate of US$60 off-peak and US$70 peak per island. The Airpass is valid for 21 days from the start of the first LIAT flight, and must be bought in Europe together with an international ticket to the Caribbean.

Turbulence

Hot weather in the Caribbean can often lead to turbulence, and if you are island hopping in small aircraft, you may experience a more bumpy ride than you are used to in larger planes. Don't worry, the turbulence rarely lasts long, and the views from the air more than make up for it.

---

island's peak season mid-December to mid-April, and during the summer from late June to mid-September. BWIA flies daily from Miami and New York to Hewanorra and George Charles, while American Eagle has daily flights between San Juan and George Charles Airport. US Airways has direct flights from Philadelphia.

From Canada — Air Canada flies from Toronto and Montreal to St Lucia. Amerijet International also flies direct during the high season.

From other Caribbean islands — LIAT, the Caribbean Airline, flies regular services between all the islands through George Charles Airport. Most flights leave early in the morning. There are flights to Anguilla, Antigua, Barbados, Barbuda, Caracas, Carriacou, Dominica, Grenada, Guadeloupe, Guyana, Martinique, Montserrat, Nevis, Port of Spain, San Juan, St Croix, St Kitts, St Maarten, St Thomas, St Vincent, Tortola and Union Island.

Air Martinique operates between Martinique and most of the Windward Islands, including St Lucia. BIAT also operates services to many of the Caribbean islands. Other operators include American Eagle, Helenair, Eagle Air and Eastern Caribbean **Helicopters**. St Lucia Helicopters is based at Pointe Seraphine. And, if you have special requirements it may pay to charter your own small aircraft.

An airport shuttle runs from Rodney Bay to the airport. One way and round trips are available! Reservations must be made ☎ 452-9329.

BY SEA

Cruise ships are regular, almost daily visitors to St Lucia. The main port of Castries and its cruise ship terminal at Pointe

(cont'd on page 12)

TOP TEN TIPS

ANSE LA RAYE
  beaches, scenery, diving

CASTRIES
  island capital, shopping,
  historic buildings

DENNERY
  fishing village

FOND ST JACQUES
  walks, scenery, wildlife

FRIGATE ISLANDS
  nature reserve

GROS ISLET
  marina, beaches, swimming

PIGEON ISLAND
NATIONAL LANDMARK
  historic site, wildlife,
  scenery

THE PITONS
  spectacular volcanic cones

POINTE DU CAP
  scenery, beaches

SOUFRIÈRE
  historic town, beaches,
  cruises, diving, Marine
  National Park

*Below: Soufrière and the Pitons
from the west coast road*

10

Above: The botanical garden at Pigeon Island National Landmark

Below: Anse La Raye and its beach

Seraphine has been modernised, and there are also port facilities at Vieux Fort and Soufrière.

Cruise lines visiting the island include Epirotiki, Holland American, Trans Ocean, Paquet, Oceanic Sunlines, Costa Lines, Fribus, Cunard, Ocean Cruise Line, Explorer Cruise Line, P&O Lines, CTC Lines, Black Sea Shipping Line, Helenic Mediterranean, Regency Clipper Cruises and Windstar Cruises.

There is now a new high speed **Catamaran service** operating between St Lucia, Martinique, Guadeloupe and Dominica, called the Caribbean Express. It calls at St Lucia twice a week and the voyage between Martinique and St Lucia takes 1 hour and 20 minutes, between Guadeloupe and St Lucia 5 hours and 40 minutes and between Dominica and St Lucia 3 hours and 25 minutes. Tickets can be booked through the travel agencies.

Hundreds of **yachts** also visit the island, and the main moorings are at Rodney Bay on the north-west coast, Castries Yacht Centre at the entrance of Castries Harbour, and Marigot Bay to the south. If you want to hitch a lift aboard one of the yachts, ask around at the marinas.

History

The Arawaks

The original people of the islands were the gentle **Arawaks**, an Amerindian race, although little is known about them or when they first arrived. They are believed to have come from Asia to South America about 40,000 years ago, and to St Lucia via Trinidad around 300BC. They fished, hunted and cultivated plants such as maize, tobacco and cassava, but food was plentiful and they had lots of time to lie in the sun and party!

They lived in small coastal communities, wore few clothes but decorated themselves with tattoos, feathers and beads, and were skilled potters.

The Caribs

The **Arawaks** were driven out by the warlike **Caribs**, another Amerindian race, some time after AD 800. They called the island Hiwanarau, later Hewanorra, the name taken by the international airport.

It is known that the Caribs had a well developed social system and common language throughout the islands. They were led by hereditary kings called 'caciques', while 'shamans' were the religious leaders. Their reputation as warriors was fearsome, and their war canoes could hold more than a hundred men able to paddle it fast enough to catch a sailing ship.

They were feared by Europeans because of horrific stories about **cannibalism** with victims being roasted on spits. The Caribs were even said to have a taste preference, thinking Frenchmen were the most tasty, and then the English and Dutch, with the Spanish considered stringy and almost inedible.

Villages were built in inland forest clearings, and each settlement had its own chieftan. Huts were round with timber walls and palm thatched roofs. Early paintings show that they enjoyed dancing, either for pleasure or as part of rituals, and they played ball games. They were primarily **fishermen and hunters**, although they did cultivate kitchen gardens, and developed a system of shift cultivation, known as 'conuco'.

The early Spanish recorded their surprise at the Arawaks' agricultural techniques, use of fibres and pottery and boat building skills. When the Caribs achieved dominance, they adopted or adapted many of the Arawak skills especially for farming and boat building, although their pottery was not as elaborate. Carib homes were rectangular and built using pole frames covered with palm thatch.

COLUMBUS

The Caribbean islands were discovered by **Columbus** in 1492 although his logs made no mention of St Lucia or any island that could be identified as it. There is a mention, however, of an island called **Martinico**. It is possible that one of Columbus's lieutenants, Juan de la Cosa, returned to the Caribbean and charted St Lucia for the first time, although his map shows an island named El Falcon where St Lucia should be. There is no evidence, though, that he landed.

St Lucia was probably first 'discovered' by Europeans around 1500, and is first mentioned in Spanish Royal Court documents in 1511. By 1520 it appeared by that name on a Vatican globe, although it is not known how it got its name. It used to be thought that Columbus discovered the island during his fourth voyage on **13 December 1502**, the feast day of St Lucia, patron saint of the

Beautiful Marigot Bay

Sicilian city of Syracuse where she was martyred in AD304. It is now known that Columbus did not discover the island, but December 13 is still celebrated as St Lucia's national day.

The island became a base for pirates during the 16th century and was the hide-out of the legendary **Francois de Clerc** in the 1550s. He was known as Jamb de Bois because of his wooden leg.

THE DUTCH

The Dutch established a base at **Vieux Fort** around 1600, but early attempts by the English at colonisation in 1605 and 1638 were unsuccessful, because of disease and the hostility of the Caribs. The 1605 landing was by accident — the English aboard the *Olive Branch* were bound for Guiana but were blown off course. Sixty-seven men came ashore and bought huts from the Caribs, but within five weeks two-thirds had been killed, and the remainder fled to sea in a dug-out canoe.

FRENCH VS ENGLISH

Ownership of the island was fiercely contested between the French and English. The French claimed possession in 1635 and in 1651 the **French West India Company** established their first settlement with a small colony from Martinique. Ten years later, they signed a treaty with the Caribs, and in 1664, a 150-year period of turmoil began when Thomas Warner, son of the Governor of St Kitts, reclaimed the island for Britain.

Over the next century and a half the island changed hands many times during repeated wars between France and England. The Caribs were also victims of this hostility and were all killed. In 1667 the island was restored to France by the **Treaty of Breda**, and in 1674 the French King claimed the island again and declared it a dependency of Martinique. In 1718 the French granted the island to Marshal d'Estrées, but this was disputed by the British crown, and in 1722 George I gave the island to the Duke of Montague. Neither side could agree a solution, and so St Lucia was declared neutral.

This 'peace' did not last for long, however, and in 1743 the French took possession of the island, and their control lasted until the **Treaty of Aix-la-Chapelle** in 1748 in which France and England again agreed that St Lucia should remain neutral. In 1746 the

French established **Soufrière** as the first town on the island, and by 1778 twelve French towns had been founded. In the interim, Admiral George Rodney and General Robert Monckton retook the island in 1762, but Britain lost it again the following year as part of the Treaty of Paris.

From 1763 French planters from Saint Vincent and Grenada established sugar and cotton plantations on the island. Over the next 15 years, more than 50 estates were established but many of these were destroyed by the 1780 hurricane, although because of slave labour, these were quickly brought back into production. In 1778 St Lucia passed into British hands when the French surrendered it after the **Battle of Cul de Sac**, and Gros Islet became an important naval base until the Treaty of Versailles in 1783 when it was again restored to France. The English fleet sailed out of Gros Islet Bay in 1790 to engage the French in the Battle of the Saints, the most decisive naval engagement ever fought in the Caribbean.

The French Revolution impacted on St Lucia. A guillotine was set up in Soufrière town square and several estate owners lost their heads to it.

Slaves were given their freedom and joined forces with troops who had deserted, and for three years they fought a guerilla battle with the English and caused widespread destruction, including the burning of Castries in 1796. The same year **General Moore** stormed the Morne defences and captured it from the French. The English referred to the guerilla band of freed slaves and deserters as the Bandits — it wasn't until 1798 that they had wrested full control of the island from them.

A British Crown Colony

Finally, in 1814 St Lucia was ceded to Britain by the **Treaty of Paris** and became a Crown Colony, in 1871 it became one of the **Windward Islands**. Between 1838-85 it was administered, along with the other Windward Islands, by the Governor of Barbados.

Slavery

During the second half of the 17th century, slaves were brought to the islands from West Africa to man the sugar cane plantations. The infamous Triangular trade was introduced — sugar and molasses from the West Indies was sent to Euro-

BEACHES

St Lucia has fabulous beaches, everything you ever dreamed of for a tropical island; golden sand, a fringe of tall palms for shade, and turquoise clear warm seas. Generally the best beaches are on the protected western coast. Beaches on the windier Atlantic Ocean coast tend to have choppier seas but offer excellent surfing and wind-surfing. Check locally for any swimming risks.

Best Beaches

Vigie beach, Reduit beach, Anse Chastanet and the beaches on Pigeon Island.

* Nude/topless bathing is illegal.

Tanning Safely

The sun is very strong, but sea breezes often disguise just how hot it is. If you are not used to the sun, take it carefully for the first two or three days, use a good sun screen with a factor of 15 or higher, and do not sunbathe during the hottest parts of the day. Wear sunglasses and a sun hat. Sunglasses will protect you against the glare, especially strong on the beach, and sun hats will protect your head. If you spend a lot of time swimming or scuba diving, take extra care as you will burn even quicker due to the combination of salt water and sun. Calamine lotion and preparations containing aloe both are useful in combating sunburn.

pean ports, and exchanged for manufactured goods which were used to buy slaves, who were sold in the West Indies for sugar.

Britain abolished the slave trade in 1807. This was three years after Haiti became the first black republic in the Americas, following the successful slave

Reduit Beach at Rodney Bay.
The public access is at the
south end of the beach

rebellion in Saint-Domingue in the late 1790s. Between 1833 and 1834, all slavery was abolished in the British West Indies. The French followed suit in 1848 and the Dutch in 1863. Just prior to slavery being abolished on the island, there were more than 13,000 slaves of African descent, 2,600 former slaves who had gained their freedom, and 2,300 whites.

AFTER EMANCIPATION

After Emancipation, however, all former slaves had to agree to serve a four year '**apprenticeship**'. They had to promise to agree working free for their former bosses for at least three quarters of their working week. The rest of the time could be spent tending small plots cleared from the forest on which crops were grown.

Without a cheap labour force after the 'apprenticeship', the plantations ceased to be profitable and the decline of the sugar cane industry set in.

Hope for economic progress during the 19th century, however, was hampered by wars, a number of serious epidemics which swept through the islands, and the continuing decline in the sugar cane industry, then the mainstay of the island's economy.

Castries, the capital, flourished in the late 1800s when it became a major coaling station. The first steamship laden with coal berthed in Port Castries in 1863, and within years, hundreds of steam ships would dock every year to take on board coal to fire their engines. Indentured Indians were brought to the island to load the ships. It became an even more important fuelling station after the opening of the Panama Canal in 1914, but the industry declined in the 1920s because of the depression and introduction of oil.

Most estates had already started to switch from sugar to banana and cacao cultivation which became dominant, and the sugar cane industry finally ended in 1964. Today tourism has overtaken agriculture as the highest foreign exchange earner.

St Lucia joined the **West Indian Federation** in 1958, enacted its own constitution in 1960, and became self ruling in 1967. It gained full independence on February 22, 1979.

GEOGRAPHY

St Lucia is of volcanic origin, and around Soufrière in the south-west, you can still see boiling bubbling mud pools and escaping sulphur and other gases from vents in the

---

The Pitons

St Lucia's 'Pyramids' in the south-west are a spectacular landmark. Gros Piton 2,619ft (798m) and Petit Piton 2,461ft (750m) are volcanic pinnacles rising out of the sea, which from a distance appear to be side by side. It is not until you drive closer that you can see just how far apart and how impressive they are with their densely forested slopes. The Pitons stand on either side of Soufrière Bay, and it is fascinating how their perspective changes as you view them from different angles as you journey around them.

The lush rain forests are now largely restricted to the higher slopes of the mountains, and are frequently only accessible on foot. Lower slopes have often been cleared for farming, and forestry is also an important island income earner.

Qualibou volcano, which last erupted in the 1780s. The volcanic crater is one of the island's main tourist attractions.

The interior of the land is wooded and mountainous with **Mount Gimie** 3,118ft (950m) the highest point. The mountains run north to south with many rivers and streams running off them through fertile valleys to east and west.

ARTS, CULTURE AND ENTERTAINMENT

St Lucians have a natural artistry which is evidenced by the wonderfully woven baskets, rugs and hats, decorated pots and ornate jewellery, often using natural material such as seeds. This artistic ability has been handed down over scores of generations, with even the earliest Arawak ceramics showing ornate patterns and designs. Canoe building and basket weaving are skills passed down ever since the Arawaks.

A craft exhibition is held every year as part of the **Independence Day** celebrations. It takes place in February and is held in either Pointe Seraphine or Castries

(cont'd on page 24)

St Lucia

Main picture: Gros Piton and Anse des Pitons from the Jalousie Hilton Plantation Resort

Right: Vincent Eudovic's studio at Goodlands

Town Hall. Today the island's artistry is best represented by painters such as the internationally-acclaimed **Llewellyn Xavier**, and the prolific **Dunstan St Omer** whose religious works adorn many of the island's Catholic churches, and potters like **Augustus Simon** and **Urmie Persaud** whose works can be found on sale in Castries.

There are innovative sculptors such as Vincent Eudovic, and poet Derek Walcott, St Lucia's 1992 Literature Nobel Laureate, who is also a fine water colour artist (the late Sir W. Arthur Lewis is the island's other Nobel Laureate, having won the prize for economics in 1979).

Soufrière is the centre of the island's natural jewellery industry, and locally produced leather goods are another example of island crafts.

Music is even more ingrained into the souls of St Lucians and pulsating rhythms blare out from cars, mini vans, homes and transistors. The music and its beat are highly infectious, and it is very easy to get carried away — go to the Gros Islet jump up and see if you can stay still for long.

Calypso celebrates news events, politics and gossip, and while it may be difficult to catch all the lyrics, you will enjoy the beat. Calypsos are sung year-round, but really come into their own at Carnival Time when the island's best vie for the title of Calypso King ☎ 452-2279.

The **Folk Research Centre** is responsible for preserving and documenting the culture and folklore of St Lucia. It has published several books on the subject, as well as cassettes and CDs. *Lucian Kaiso* is published annually and documents each calypso season, while *A Handbook for Writing Creole* explains the main features of Antillean Creole. If you are interested in reading more about the island and its folk-lore, buy a copy of *Annou Di-Y An Kweyol*, a collection of folk tales with texts in Creole and English. A copy of the *Dictionary of St Lucian Creole* might also come in handy.

Musical Traditions of St Lucia is an album of 32 selections which represent all the musical genres found on the island. More information from the Folk Research Centre, PO Box 514, Mount Pleasant, Castries (☎ 809-452-2279).

Bridging the gap between culture and entertainment is cricket, played by almost everyone, anytime and anywhere. If you get the chance, go and watch a match being played at the Mindoo Phillips Cricket Ground. It is an experience you will never forget.

CLIMATE

Any time is a good time to visit St Lucia. The **high season** is generally regarded as between mid-November and March, the driest months, but the island now attracts visitors by air and from cruise ships year round. Most rain falls between May and October.

St Lucia enjoys a marvellous climate and even when it does rain, it is warm rain and generally does not last long. The island lies within the tropical zone in the path of the northeast trade winds and has a typical sub-tropical maritime climate of year-round sunny, warm weather.

Temperatures remain fairly constant throughout the year, with only a few degrees fluctuation between summer and winter. **Average daytime temperatures** are around 85°F (29°) and average night temperatures around 65° (18°C). During the hottest part of the year between June and August, however, temperatures can of-

ten be in the high nineties.

Frost is unusual even at the highest mountain altitudes, and humidity rarely rises above 85 per cent because of onshore breezes.

Average annual rainfall ranges from around 51 inches (130cm) on the coast to around 150 inches (381cm) in the rain forests of the mountainous interior. The **dry season** lasts from January to April, but do not be fooled into thinking it doesn't rain during these months. The best season is from May to November.

Average temperature is about 80°F (27°C), although the temperature can reach 88°F (31°C) during the summer and fall to around 66°F (19°C) in the winter. The sea breezes prevent temperatures from rising or falling dramatically, and provide air movement so that one rarely feels too hot.

St Lucia was badly hit in 1980 by Hurricane Allen which destroyed much of the island's infrastructure, wiped out crops and seriously hit tourism. Fortunately, however, St Lucia has had far fewer hurricanes than most other islands in the Caribbean.

THE ST LUCIAN PARROT

Since the 1970s, great efforts have been made to protect the St Lucian parrot, and five St Lucians, all employed by the Forestry Department, were trained in conservation at Jersey Zoo under the late Gerald Durrell. At the end of the 1970s it was thought that there were less than 100 St Lucian parrots in the wild. In 1976, a number of birds were captured and sent to Jersey to start a breeding programme.

A major conservation effort has also been under way to restore the threatened parrot's habitat, and an environmental awareness campaign has been taking place in the island's schools to educate the children about the importance of protecting the countryside and the wildlife living in it.

THE PEOPLE

The overwhelming majority of the population are of African descent, their ancestors having been brought to the island as slaves. Less than a tenth are of mixed European and black African blood; a small percentage are Asians and Europeans.

The **French influence** remains strong both in many of the island's names and in the island's predominant religion. Most people are Roman Catholics, although there are also many churches of various Protestant faiths, especially Seventh Day Adventists and Anglicans. The official language is English, but because of the historic influence of the French, a French patois (a dialect of creole) is largely spoken. Castries is the capital and main population centre, with Soufrières and Vieux Fort, the other main towns. Just over half the population lives in rural communities, but there is a steady move towards urban areas.

St Lucia has a young population with more than a third of the population under the age of 15 years, and two-thirds under the age of 30 years. The population is about 158,000 and expected to reach 177,000 by 2010.

Above: Anse La Raye
Below: Pointe Seraphine and Choc Bay

THE ECONOMY

The island's economy is based on farming, fishing, forestry and tourism. The gross national product is growing more rapidly than the population, and is one of the most buoyant in the Caribbean.

Most of the cultivated land is divided into small farms of a few acres, and bananas are by far the most important crop accounting for almost two-thirds of agricultural exports. Other cash crops include cacao, coconuts, citrus fruits and spices, while subsistence crops include cassava, yams, plantains, mangoes and papaya.

Manufacturing has traditionally been based on processing agricultural produce, but was diversified after Hurricane Allen with the construction of factories to produce electrical components, cardboard cartons, clothing, rum, tobacco products, coconut products, beer and concrete blocks. An oil refinery transhipment complex was built at Cul de Sac Bay in the late 1970s. There is an industrial free zone near Vieux Fort producing electronic goods and toys for export. Tourism has developed rapidly in the last 25 years, and the cruise ship complex in Castries was opened in December 1986.

Main imports are food, fuels, farm chemicals and machinery, and other manufactured goods. The island's main trading partners are the UK, United States, Trinidad and Tobago and Barbados. Tourism has flourished since 1970; it is now the main industry, and continues to grow in economic importance.

POLITICS

Representative government was granted by the constitution in 1924, and the constitution of 1936 allowed for an unofficial majority of elected representatives in the legislative council.

St Lucia was a member of the Federation of the West Indies between 1958 and 1962, and in 1960 the post of Governor of the Windward Islands was abolished and Saint Lucia became an autonomous unit with-in the Federation until its abolition in May, 1962. On 1 March 1967, under the **West Indies Act**, St Lucia became fully self-governing, responsible for all its internal affairs, although the United Kingdom retained responsibility for defence and external affairs.

Constitution

Saint Lucia is a constitutional monarchy and a member of the Commonwealth. **Queen Elizabeth II** is head of state and is represented in the country by an appointed Governor-General. The head of Government is the Prime Minister, who is leader of the majority party. The Parliament has two chambers, the **House of Assembly** with 17 seats, whose members are elected for five years, and the **Senate**, with 11 seats, whose members are generally appointed on the advice of the Prime Minister, leader of the Opposition and the Governor-General.

Finally, the island gained full independence on 22 February 1979. The United Workers Party (UWP) was in power and called new elections, but was defeated by the Saint Lucia Labour Party (SLP). The two have vied for power ever since, and the UWP was returned to power in 1982 and again, by a narrow majority in 1987.

The UWP, led by John Compton, was returned to office again in April, 1992 with an 11-6 majority in the House of Assembly and 56.3 per cent of the vote. Compton, who was also Prime Minister before Independence and headed successive governments between 1964 and 1979, retired in 1996 and was succeeded by Vaughan Lewis. In the May 1997 general election the UWP was trounced and the SLP won 16 of the 17 seats and lawyer Kenny Anthony was sworn in as Prime Minister. He was re-elected in 2001.

The major problem facing the country is high unemployment coupled with population growth. These conditions, together with inflation and relatively high living costs, have led to considerable political unrest.

The Government provides health facilities for the people and there are hospital facilities in Castries, Vieux Fort, Soufrière and Dennery, with health centres and pharmacies in many of the smaller com-munties. There is also a private hospital run by a religious order at Vieux Fort.

Primary education is free and compulsory, and many of the primary schools are parochial and run by the Catholic church. There is a general faculty of the **University of the West Indies** in Castries. There is also a teacher training college and technical college on the island.

Main picture: Cul de Sac Valley from Vincent Eudovic's studio

Left: Coconuts ready for processing, Morne Coubaril Estate

Saint Lucia has retained its association with the Eastern Caribbean Supreme Court, and has a Court of Appeal and High Court.

THE MEDIA

There are two island radio stations — **Radio St Lucia** which broadcasts music, local news and current affairs, and **Radio Caribbean International**. The two local television stations are HTS-Channel 4 which broadcasts nightly news and current affairs, and DBS. Satellite also allows a number of American channels to be shown. The island also has several newspapers. *The Voice* is the main newspaper, which is published three times a week. The three weekly newspapers are *The Star*, *The Crusader* and *The Mirror*.

FLORA & FAUNA

The lush vegetation and animal life are part of the island's great charm. There are palms of all descriptions, giant ferns, bamboos, bananas, coconut groves, hanging breadfruit, mango, nutmeg, cocoa, pawpaw and the most stunning array of spectacularly coloured flowering plants from giant African tulip trees festooned with scarlet blossoms to tiny orchids. Bougainvillea flowers everywhere, there are scores of varieties of hibiscus, frangipani and poinsettia. There are heliconia, also known as the lobster plant, bird of paradise flowers and anthurium everywhere. The flamboyant tree is also known as the tourist tree because it bursts into bloom during the summer and is a blaze of colour.

Along the coast you can find swamps, mangroves and marsh woodlands, while inland there are breathtaking walks through tropical rain forests. Beach morning glory with its array of pink flowers is found on many beaches, and is important because its roots help prevent sand drift. The plant also produces nectar from glands in the base of its leaf stalks which attract ants, and it is thought this evolution has occurred so that the ants will discourage any leaf-nibbling predators. Other beach plants include seagrape and the manchineel, which should be treated with caution.

Coastal swamps also provide a rich habitat for wildlife. Tiny tree crabs and burrowing edible land crabs scurry around in the mud trapped in the roots

Underwater

Of course, the sea teems with brilliantly coloured fish and often, even more spectacularly coloured coral and marine plants. Even if you just float upside down in the water with a face mask on, you will be able to enjoy many of the beautiful underwater scenes, but the best way to see things is by scuba diving, snorkelling or taking a trip in one of the many glass bottomed boats.

There are scores of different multi-coloured corals that make up the reefs offshore. There are hard and soft corals and only one, the fire coral poses a threat to swimmers and divers, because if touched, it causes a stinging skin rash. Among the more spectacular corals are deadman's fingers, staghorn, brain coral and seafans, and there are huge sea anemones and sponges, while tropical fish species include the parrotfish, blue tang surgeonfish, tiny but aggressive damselfish, angelfish and brightly coloured wrasse.

of mangrove trees just above water level. Herons, egrets, pelicans and often frigatebirds roost in the higher branches. The mangrove cuckoo shares the lower branches with belted kingfishers.

Inland, gardens are generally a blaze of colour with flowers in bloom year round, growing alongside exotic vegetables like yam, sweet potato, and dasheen. Flowering plants include the flamboyant tree with their brilliant red flowers which burst into bloom in early summer, and long dark brown seed pods, which can be used as rattles when the seeds have dried out inside.Occasionally flamboyants have yellow blossoms but this is

rare. Bougainvillea grows everywhere and seems to be in bloom year round in a host of different colours. In fact, the colour does not come from petals but the plant's bract-like leaves which surround the small petal-less flowers. There are yellow and purple allamandas, poinsettia, hibiscus, anthurium and multi-coloured flowers of the ixora.

The leaves of the travellers palm spread out like a giant open fan, and the tree got its name because the fan was believed to point from south to north.

The flowers attract hummingbirds like the doctorbird, as well as the carib grackle, a

Above left: The ginger lily
Above right: Pineapples growing at Invergoll Estate
Below: Exotic tropical flowers abound all over the island

A NOTE OF WARNING – THE MANCHINEEL

The manchineel can be found on many beaches and has a number of effective defensive mechanisms which can prove very painful. Trees vary from a few feet to more than 30ft (9m) in height, and have widely spreading, deep forked boughs with small, dark green leaves and yellow stems, and fruit like small, green apples.

If you examine the leaves carefully without touching them, you will notice a small pin-head sized raised dot at the junction of leaf and leaf stalk. The apple-like fruit is very poisonous, and sap from the tree causes very painful blisters. It is so toxic that early Caribs are said to have dipped their arrow heads in it before hunting trips. Sap is released if a leaf or branch is broken, more so after rain. Avoid contact with the tree, do not sit under it or on a fallen branch, and do not eat the fruit. If you do get sap on your skin, run into the sea and wash it off as quickly as possible.

strutting, starling like bird with a paddle-shaped tail, and friendly bananaquit. You can also spot tree lizards, and the larger geckos which hunt at night.

Along **roadsides and hedge-rows** in the countryside, you can see the vinelike caralita, calabash with its gourd-like fruits, tamarind and distinctive star-shaped leaves of the castor bean, whose seeds when crushed yield castor oil.

Areas of **scrubland** have their own flora or fauna, with plants bursting into colour following the first heavy rains after the dry season. There are century plants, with their prickly, sword like leaves, which grows for up to twenty years before flowering. The yellow flower stalk grows at a tremendous rate for several days and can reach 20ft (6m) high, but having bloomed once the whole plant then dies.

Other typical scrubland vegetation includes aloe, acacia,

prickly pear and several species of cactus. Fiddlewood provides hard timber for furniture, highly coloured variegated crotons, the white flowered, aromatic frangipani and sea island cotton which used to provide the very finest cotton. Scrub vegetation also plays host to birds such as the mockingbird, ground dove, kingbird and grassquit, and it is the ideal habitat for lizards.

The rain forests which cover 19,000 acres provide the most prolific vegetation with mahogany trees with their fascinating black and red seeds, much used for necklaces. There are magnificent swathes of giant ferns, towering bamboo groves, enormous air plants, and a host of flowering or variegated plants such as heliconia, philodendron and wild fuchsia. There are balsa wood trees, the world's lightest wood, the flowering vine marcgravia, the prolific mountain cabbage palm and among the foliage and flowers you can find hummingbirds and parrots.

Animal Life

The animal life on the island is not diverse and there are few large animals. There are frogs and toads which croak loudly all night, lizards and snakes such as the poisonous fer-de-lance, introduced by the plantation owners and kept in perimeter ditches round the estate to deter slaves from escaping.

Mongooses, which grow up to two feet in length including tail, were said to have been first introduced to the islands to kill rats gnawing at the sugar cane. There is also a story that they were introduced to kill the fer-de-lance. There is one species of lizard, the Zandoli Te, which is unique to the Maria Islands, two small islands off the south-east coast of St Lucia. These islands are protected as a nature reserve. Attempts are being made to introduce the lizard to other offshore islands to try to improve its chances of survival. The agouti is common. There are also a few boa constrictors.

Another unusual animal is the **manicou**, St Lucia's opossum, introduced to the island from Dominica in 1902. It lives in trees, forages over huge areas at night, and is not averse to rooting through trash cans for any delicacies.

Lumbering sea turtles also come ashore at night between March and August to lay their eggs in the sand. There are butterflies and less attractive insects such as mosquitoes, ants and sand flies.

BIRDS

There is, however, a remarkably rich and colourful native bird life, including the threatened **St Lucian parrot**, the island's national symbol, the Saint Lucia Oriole, white breated thrashers Peewee and the Saint Lucia black finch. There are also mangrove cuckoos, humming birds, tanagers, ibis, mocking birds, herons, egrets and many others.

Offshore you may sight the magnificent **frigate bird**, easily recognisable by its size, long black 7ft (2m) wing span, forked tail and apparently effortless ability to glide on the winds. There are brown booby birds, named by sailors from the Spanish word for 'fool' because they were so easy to catch. Pelicans which look so ungainly on land, yet are so acrobatic in the air, are common, as are laughing gulls and royal terns. Several species of sandpiper can usually be seen scurrying around at the water's edge.

If you are really interested in bird watching, pack a small pair of binoculars. Mini-binoculars are ideal for island bird watching, because the light is normally so good that you will get a clear image despite the small object lens. The best bird watching is in the Bois D'orange swamp, Rain Forests and Boriel's Pond. Contact the Forest and Lands Department for organised tours of the Rain Forest. ☎ 450-2231

PLANTS, ETC

As most of the plants, fruits, vegetables and spices will be new to the first time visitor, the following brief descriptions are offered.

BANANAS

Bananas are still one of the island's most important exports, earning EC$126 million in 1997. Although exports have declined, bananas are still known as 'green gold', and grow everywhere.

There are three types of banana plant; the banana that we normally buy in supermarkets originated in Malaya and were introduced into the Caribbean in the early 16th century by the Spanish. The large bananas, or **plantains**, originally came from southern India, and are largely used in cooking. They are often fried and served as an accompaiment to fish and meat. The third variety is the **red banana**, which is not grown commercially, but which can be seen around the island.

Most banana plantations cover only a few acres and are worked by the owner or tenant, although there are still some very large holdings. A banana produces a crop about very nine months, and each cluster of flowers grows into a hand of bananas. A bunch can contain up to twenty hands of bananas, with each hand having up to 20 individual fruit.

Although they grow tall, bananas are not trees but herbacious plants which die back each year. Once the plant has produced fruit, a shoot from the ground is cultivated to take its place, and the old plant dies. Bananas need a lot of attention, and island farmers will tell you that there are not enough hours in a day to do everything that needs to be

Captain Bligh

Breadfruit was introduced to the Caribbean by **Captain Bligh** in 1793. He brought 1,200 breadfruit saplings from Tahiti aboard the Providence. These were first planted in Jamaica and St Vincent, and then quickly spread throughout the islands.

It was Bligh's attempts to bring in young breadfruit trees that led to the mutiny on the **Bounty** four years earlier. Bligh was given the command of the 215-ton *Bounty* in 1787 and was ordered to take the bread fruit trees from Tahiti to the West Indies where they were to be used to provide cheap food for the slaves. The ship had collected its cargo and had reached Tonga when the crew under **Fletcher Christian** mutinied. The crew claimed that Bligh's regime was too tyranical, and he and 18 members of the crew who stayed loyal to him were cast adrift in an open boat. The cargo of breadfruit was dumped overboard.

Bligh, in a remarkable feat of seamanship, navigated the boat for 3,600 miles (5,796km) until making landfall on **Timor** in the East Indies. Some authorities have claimed that it was the breadfruit tree cargo that sparked the mutiny, as each morning the hundreds of trees in their heavy containers had to be carried on deck, and then carried down into the hold at nightfall. It might have proved just too much for the already overworked crew.

Rodney Bay marina

done. The crop needs fertilising regularly, leaves need cutting back, and you will often see the fruit protected inside blue tinted plastic containers, which protect it from insect and bird attack, and speed up maturation.

BREADFRUIT

Breadfruit is a cheap carbohydrate-rich food, although pretty tasteless when boiled. It is best eaten fried, baked or roasted over charcoal. The slaves did not like them, but the tree spread and can now be found almost everywhere. It has large dark, green leaves, and the large green fruits can weigh 10-12lbs (4-5kg). The falling fruit explode with a loud bang and splatter their pulpy contents over a large distance. It is said that no one goes hungry when the breadfruit are in season.

CALABASH TREES

Calabash trees are native to the Caribbean and have huge gourd-like fruits which are very versatile when dried and cleaned. They can be used as water containers, bowls, bailers for boats and as lanterns. Juice from the pulp is boiled into a concentrated syrup and used to treat coughs and colds, the fruit is said to have many other medicinal uses. The calabash is St Lucia's national tree.

COCOA

Cocoa is another important crop — its Latin name *theobroma* means 'food of the gods'. A cocoa tree can produce several thousand flowers a year, but only a fraction of these will develop into seed bearing pods. It is the heavy orange pods hanging from the cocoa tree which contain the beans bearing the seeds that produce cocoa and chocolate. The beans containing a sweet, white sap that protects the seeds which are split open and kept in trays to ferment. This process takes up to eight days and the seeds must be kept at a regular temperature to ensure the right flavour and aroma develops. The seeds are then dried.

In the old days people used to walk barefoot over the beans to polish them to enhance their appearance. Today the beans are crushed to extract cocoa butter, and the remaining powder is cocoa. Real chocolate is produced by mixing cocoa powder, cocoa butter and sugar.

You can buy **cocoa balls** or rolls like fat chocolate fingers in the markets, which make a delicious drink. Each ball is the size of a large cherry. Simply dissolve the ball in a pan of boiling water, allow to simmer and then add sugar and milk or cream for a rich chocolate drink. Each ball will make about four mugs of chocolate.

COCONUT PALMS

Coconut palms are everywhere and should be treated with caution. Anyone who has heard the whoosh of a descending coconut knows how scary the sound is. Very few people are injured by falling cocounts, a near miracle in view of the tens of thousands of palms all over the island. However it is not a good idea to picnic in a coconut grove!

Coconut trees are incredibly hardy, able to grow in sand even when regularly washed by salty sea water. They can also survive long periods without rain. Their huge leaves, up to 20ft (6m) long in mature trees, drop down during dry spells so a smaller surface area is exposed to the sun which reduces evaporation. Coconut palms can grow up to 80ft (26m) tall, and produce up to 100 seeds a year. The seeds are the second largest in the plant kingdom.

The coconut husk

The coconut that we all traditionally buy is the seed with its layer of coconut surrounded by a hard shell. This shell is then surrounded by a layer of copra, a fibrous material, and this is covered by a large green husk. The seed and protective coverings can weigh 30lbs (13kg) and more. The seed and casing is waterproof, drought proof and able to float. This explains why coconut palms which originated in the Pacific and Indian Oceans are now found throughout the Caribbean — the seeds literally floated across the seas.

The coconut palm is extremely versatile. The leaves can be used as thatch for roofing or cut into strips and woven into mat and baskets, while the husks yield coir, a fibre resistant to salt water and ideal for ropes, brushes and brooms. Green coconuts contain a delicious thirst-quenching 'milk', and the coconut 'meat' can be eaten raw or baked in ovens for two days before being sent to processing plants where the oil is extracted. Coconut oil is used in cooking, soaps, synthetic

A NOTE OF WARNING –
PEPPER SAUCE - HOT OR HOTTER?

On most tables you will find a bottle of pepper sauce. It usually contains a blend of several types of hot pepper, spices and vinegar and should be treated cautiously. Try a little first before splashing it all over your food, as these sauces range from hot to unbearable.

If you want to make your own hot pepper sauce, take four ripe hot peppers, one teaspoon each of oil, ketchup and vinegar, add a pinch of salt, blend together into a liquid, and bottle.

rubber and even in hydraulic brake fluid.

As you drive around the island, you will see groups of men and women splitting the coconuts in half with machetes, preparing them for the ovens. You might also see halved coconut shells spaced out on the corrugated tin roofs of some homes. These are being dried before being sold to the copra processing plants.

DASHEEN

Dasheen is one of the crops known as 'ground provisions' in the islands, the others being potatoes, yams, eddo and tannia. The last two are close relatives of dasheen, and all are members of the aroid family, some of the world's oldest cultivated crops. Dasheen (with its 'elephant ear' leaves), and eddo grow from a corm which when boiled thoroughly can be used like potato, and the young leaves of either are used to make calaloo, a spinach-like soup. Both dasheen and eddo are thought to have come from China or Japan. Tannia is native to the Caribbean and its roots can be boiled, baked or fried.

GUAVA

Guava is common throughout the islands — the aromatic, pulpy fruit is also a favourite with birds who then distribute its seeds. The fruit-bearing shrub can be seen on roadsides and in gardens, and it is used to make a wide range of products from jelly to 'cheese', a paste

Above: Roseau Bay

Below: Snapped near Dennery

made by mixing the fruit with sugar. The fruit which range from a golf ball to a tennis ball in size, is a rich source of vitamin A and contains lots more vitamin C than citrus fruit.

MANGO

Mango can be delicious if somewhat messy to eat. They originally came from India but are now grown throughout the Caribbean and found wherever there are people. Young mangoes can be stringy and unappetising, but ripe fruit from mature trees which grow up to 50ft (15m) and more, are usually delicious and can be eaten raw or cooked. The juice is a great reviver in the morning, and the fruit is often used to make jams and other preserves. The wood of the mango is often used by boatbuilders.

PASSION FRUIT

Passion fruit is not widely grown but it can usually be bought at the market. The pulpy fruit contains hundreds of tiny seeds, and many people prefer to press the fruit and drink the juice. It is also commonly used in fruit salads, sherbets and ice creams.

PAWPAW TREES

Pawpaw trees are also found throughout the island and are commonly grown in gardens. The trees are prolific fruit producers but grow so quickly that

Nutmeg

Nutmeg trees are found on all the islands. St Lucia is one of the world's top producers, although the price farmers get has crashed so much in recent years that it is sometimes not economic to gather the crop. The tree thrives in hilly, wet areas and the fruit is the size of a small tomato.

The outer husk, which splits open while still on the tree, is used to make the very popular nutmeg jelly. Inside the seed is protected by a bright red casing which, when dried and crushed, produces the spice mace. Finally, the dark outer shell of the seed is broken open to reveal the nutmeg which is dried and then ground into a powder, or sold whole so that it can be grated to add flavour to dishes.

the fruit soon becomes difficult to gather. The large, juicy melon-like fruits are eaten fresh, pulped for juice or used locally to make jams, preserves and ice cream. They are rich sources of vitamin A and C.

The leaves and fruit contain an enzyme which tenderises meat, and tough joints cooked wrapped in pawpaw leaves or covered in slices of fruit, usually taste like more expensive cuts. The same enzyme, papain, is also used in chewing gum, cosmetics, the tanning industry and in making wool shrink-resistant. A tea made from unripe fruit is said to be good for lowering high blood pressure.

Pigeon Peas

Pigeon Peas are widely cultivated and can be found in many back gardens. The plants are very hardy and drought resistant, with prolific yields of peas which can be eaten fresh or dried and used in soups and stews.

Pineapples

Pineapples were certainly grown in the Caribbean by the time Columbus arrived, and were probably brought from South America by the Amerindians. The fruit is slightly smaller than the Pacific pineapple, but the flavour more intense.

Sugar Apple

Sugar Apple is a member of the annona fruit family, and grows wild and in gardens throughout the islands. The small, soft sugar apple fruit can be peeled off in strips when ripe, and is like eating thick apple sauce. They are eaten fresh or used to make sherbet or drinks. Soursop is a member of the same family, and its spiny fruits can be seen in hedgerows and gardens. They are eaten fresh or used for preserves, drinks and ice cream.

Sugar Cane

Sugar Cane is no longer grown commercially but can still be seen growing. The canes can grow up to 12ft (4m) tall and, after cutting, the canes have to be crushed to extract the sugary juice. Most estates had their own sugar mill powered by water wheels or windmills. The remains of many of these mills can still be seen around the island, and much of the original machinery, mostly made in Britain, is still in place. After extraction, the juice is boiled until the sugar crystalised. The mixture remaining is molasses and this is used to produce rum.

FOOD AND DRINK

FOOD

Dining out in the Caribbean offers the chance to experiment with all sorts of unusual spices, vegetables and fruits, with creole and island dishes and, of course, rum punches and other exotic cocktails.

Many hotels have a tendency to offer buffet dinners or barbecues, but even these can be interesting and tasty affairs.

Eating out is generally very relaxed, and few restaurants have a strict dress code, although most people like to wear some-thing a little smarter at dinner after a day on the beach or out sightseeing.

LUNCH

Lunches are best eaten at beach cafes which usually offer excellent barbecued fresh fish and conch — which often appears on menus as lambi (not to be confused for lamb). Lobster and crab are also widely available. Dishes are mostly served with local vegetables such as fried plantain, cassava and yam. Fresh fruit such as pineapple, mango, golden apple or papaya make an ideal and light dessert.

DINNER

There is an enormous choice when it comes to dinner.

Starters include traditional Caribbean dishes such as Christophene and coconut soup, and Callaloo soup made from the leaves of dasheen, a spinach-like vegetable. There is also a strong French tradition with such dishes as soupe Germou made from pumpkin and garlic, and pouile dudon, a chicken stew with coconut and molasses. Fish and clam chowders are also popular starters. Try heart of palm, excellent fresh shrimps or scallops, smoked kingfish wrapped in crepes or crab backs, succulent land crab meat sauteed with breadcrumbs and seasoning, and served restuffed in the shell. It is much sweeter than the meat of sea crabs.

The fish is generally excellent, and don't be alarmed if you see dolphin on the menu. It is not the protected species made famous by 'Flipper' but a solid, close-textured flat faced fish called dorado, which is delicious. There is also tuna, snapper, lobster, swordfish, baby squid and mussels.

Above: One of the colonial style properties on the Morne

Right: Pointe Seraphine Shopping Centre

Below: The Royal St Lucian Hotel

Try seafood jambalaya, chunks of lobster, shrimps and ham served on a bed of braised seasoned rice, shrimp creole, with fresh shrimp sauted in garlic butter and parsley and served with tomatoes, or fish creole, with fresh fish steaks cooked in a spicy onion, garlic and tomato sauce and served with rice and fried plaintain. Other island specialities include sauted scallops with ginger, curried fish steaks lightly fried with a curry sauce and served with sliced bananas, cucumber, fresh coconut and rice.

It seems such a waste to travel to the Caribbean and eat burgers and steaks, especially when there are many much more exciting meat dishes available.

You could try curried chicken served in a coconut shell, curried goat, gingered chicken with mango and spices, Caribbean souse, with cuts of lean pork marinated with shredded cucumber, onions, garlic, lime juice and peppersauce.

For **vegetarians** there are excellent salads, stuffed breadfruit, callaloo bake, stuffed squash and pawpaw, baked sweet potato and yam casserole.

For **dessert**, try fresh fruit salad, or one of the exotically flavoured ice creams. There are also banana fritters and banana flambe, coconut cheesecake and tropical fruit sorbets.

Most menus and dishes are self-explanatory, but one or two things are worth bearing in mind. When green fig appears on the menu, it usually means green banana, which is peeled and boiled as a vegetable. It is one half of St Lucia's national dish: green fig and salt fish. Salt fish used to be salted cod, but now it can be any fish.

BUFFET

On the buffet table, you will often see a dish called pepper pot. This is usually a hot, spicy meat and vegetable stew to which may be added small flour dumplings and shrimps.

There are wonderful breads in the Caribbean which you should try if you get the chance. There are banana and pumpkin breads, and delicious cakes such as coconut loaf cake, guava jelly cookies and rum cake.

Do not be afraid to eat out. Food is often prepared in front of you, and there are some excellent snacks available from island eateries. Try deep fried cakes of dough called floats, or saltfish, corned beef fritters and coconut patties.

You must try roti, an East Indian creation which is available almost everywhere. It is a paper-thin dough wrapped round a spicy, hot curry mixture, and contains beef, chicken, vegetables or fish. The chicken roti often contains bones which some people like to chew on — be warned.

DRINK

Rum is the Caribbean drink. There are almost as many rums in the West Indies as there are malt whiskies in Scotland, and there is an amazing variety of strength, colour and quality. Learn more about the history of rum by taking the Rhythm of Rum tour at St Lucia Distillers' operation in the Roseau Valley. Enjoy a distillery tour and tasting. ☎ 451-4258.

The finest rums are best drunk on the rocks, but if you want to capture a bit of the Caribbean spirit, have a couple of rum punches.

The local beer is Piton, available on both tap and in bottles and it is very good.

To make **Plantation Rum Punch,** thoroughly mix 3 ounces of rum, with one ounce of lime juice and one teaspoon of honey, then pour over crushed ice, and add a pinch of freshly grated nutmeg.

Most hotels and bars also offer a wide range of cocktails both alcoholic, usually very strong, and non-alcoholic. Beer, drunk cold and from the bottle, is the most popular drink, and wine, where available, is often expensive because of taxes, and the choice limited.

Tap water is safe to drink as are ice cubes made from it. Mineral, bottled water and soft drinks are widely available.

> **Note**: While many of the restaurants do offer excellent service, time does not always have the same urgency as it does back home, and why should it after all, as you are on holiday. Relax, enjoy a drink, the company and the surroundings and don't worry if things take just a little longer. The wait is generally worth it.

Castries

The island's capital is a charming, bustling city which gives little indication of its long and troubled past. Castries has seen more than its fair share of action over the past 300 years as nations fought over it, and natural disasters destroyed it.

In the past 200 years, Castries has been hit by four massive fires, the first in 1796 largely as a result of the French Revolution when French Revolutionary agents incited the slaves to rebel against the English. There were also fires in 1812 and 1927, and the last in 1948 wiped out almost all the commercial quarter. Each has resulted in massive rebuilding. The fires did spare, however, a number of wonderful old wooden buildings, with

Below: Reduit Beach

their shaded overhanging balconies and delicate filigree latticework.

On the outskirts of town as the houses hug the hillsides, you can see typical Caribbean **gingerbread structures**, many supported by poles and pillars. The fires had the added advantage that each time the city needed to be rebuilt, planners could use the latest techniques, and this explains its modern grid lay out, which makes it very easy to explore, and the large number of concrete buildings.

Castries is also a city of contrasts with its ultra modern cruise ship terminal at **Pointe Seraphine** with its duty free shopping and tourist centre, and the crowded sidewalks of the streets overflowing with produce and goods from the tightly packed stores. In 1890 Castries had a population of 8,000, today the city and surroundings is home to six times this number.

CASTRIES BY FOOT

The only way to see Castries is by foot, and a good place to start is in **Derek Walcott Square** with its war memorial and 19th century iron railings. It contains the busts of the islands two Nobel laureates, Sir Arthur Lewis, who was awarded the Nobel Prize for Economics in 1979 and Derek Walcott who won the Nobel Prize for Literature in 1992. On the eastern side of the square across Laborie Street is the **Roman Catholic Cathedral of the Immaculate Conception.** Built in 1897 it contains many paintings of Biblical scenes in which all the characters are black.

Next to the cathedral is a massive **saman tree**, believed to be one of the oldest trees in the Caribbean, and certainly the oldest on St Lucia. The tree, sometimes known as a rain tree, is at least 400 years old.

On the opposite side of the square is the main **library** housed in an impressive Victorian building, while the other two sides contain a number of charming old French wooden buildings, with their latticework and balconies which have been carefully restored.

The main downtown **shopping area** is bordered by Jeremie Street in the north, Mandel Street in the west, Peynier Street in the east and Brazil Street in the south. Within this area you will find scores of shops and mini markets to explore, offering a huge range of goods from fresh fruit, vegetables and spices, to island handicrafts, and from antique prints to the latest books and records.

Of interest is the **Artsibit Gallery** on the corner of Brazil and Mongiraud Streets, which sells paintings, pottery, sculpture, prints and posters. The Book Salon on the corner of Jeremie and Laborie Streets has books, maps and stationery, while J.Q. Charles on Bridge Street and William Peter Boulevard is useful for hardware and electrical supplies. Gift shops include Cox & Co on William Peter Boulevard, Mystique Gift Shop in Laborie Street, Noah's Arkade on Jeremie Street, and the Sea Island Cotton Shop on Bridge Street.

If you want detailed maps of the island these can be obtained from the Lands and Surveys Department opposite Barclays Bank in Jeremie Street. If you want to explore some of the smaller roads inland, an ordnance survey map is strongly recommended.

The Market

After browsing the shops, visit the new EC\$8.7 million indoor fruit and vegetable **market** on Peynier Street looking out over the harbour. On your way, notice the **Court House** on the left of Peynier Street, next to the small Constitution Park, and the **Town Hall** just beyond on the right. Although the red roofed market buildings are new, the market still offers the same produce as it has for the last 200 years. The old market used to flood so often that locals thought it should have been the fish market. The new market has space for 760 vendors, who offer fresh fruits, vegetables and spices of all descriptions, and on Saturday, the busiest day, the market is swelled by people from outlying villages coming to sell their produce.

As you enter the market, you are likely to be greeted by a **market guide**, either official or freelance, and it may help to make use of their services on your first visit in return for a small tip. They will identify the various produce for you and can explain what they are used for. The old 19th century vegetable market with its large red gates, has been totally renovated and the floor raised.It now houses the crafts market with outlets for more than 600 producers offering woven baskets, mats, pottery, wood carvings, jewellery and other island produce.

Explore the streets behind the market as there are fascinating alleys packed with tiny eateries serving island specialities and snacks. You can sit out on the narrow streets, enjoy some real St Lucia fare and let life pass you by for a few minutes.

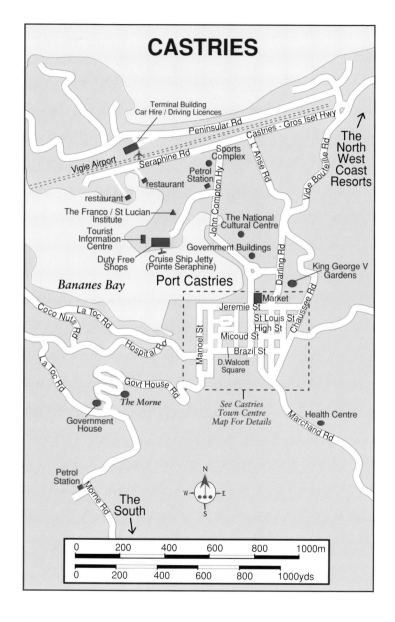

CASTRIES

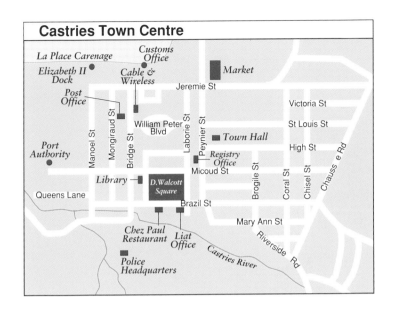

Castries Town Centre

La Place Carenage

Customs Office

Elizabeth II Dock

Market

Cable & Wireless

Jeremie St

Post Office

Victoria St

Manoel St

Mongiraud St

Bridge St

William Peter Blvd

Laborie St

Peynier St

St Louis St

Town Hall

High St

Port Authority

Registry Office

Micoud St

Brogile St

Coral St

Chisel St

Chauss e Rd

Library

D.Walcott Square

Queens Lane

Brazil St

Mary Ann St

Chez Paul Restaurant

Liat Office

Castries River

Riverside Rd

Police Headquarters

Below left: The Roman Catholic Cathedral, built in 1897

Right: This saman tree in D.Walcott Square is over 400 years old

ALONG JOHN COMPTON HIGHWAY

You can then walk along the **John Compton Highway** which hugs the harbour out of Castries to visit **Pointe Seraphine** and the cruise ship terminal. The road passes the **Government Offices** on the right, and you take the first turning on your left past the fish market to reach the terminal. The strange white pointed building with its steeply sloping roof, as you approach the terminal, is the home of the Alliance Francaise.

If there is a cruise ship docked, you can stand alongside and marvel at just how large these vessels are. Helicopters often land behind the duty free complex ferrying passengers around the island. There are a number of up-market duty free boutiques at **Pointe Seraphine** as well as the main tourist information office, and the headquarters of the tourist board. Shops include Colombian Emeralds International, Harry Edwards Jewelers, Timbuktoo (funky fashions), Just Leather, Raffles, Oasis, Peer, Coco Joe's Beach Shack.

Inexpensive $ Moderate $$ *Expensive $$$* The * system (from one to four) is based on quality of food, service and ambience.

Auberge Seraphine Restaurant
(☎ 453-2073)
Overlooks Vigie yacht marina. Open daily for breakfast, lunch and dinner offering a varied menu of Caribbean and international cuisine. Happy hour 5 – 6.30pm. Dinner reservations recommended.

Burger Plus $ *
St Louis Street
(☎ 452-7587)
A fast food eatery offering chicken, fish, burgers, fries and soft drinks.

Caribbees $$ ***
(☎ 452-4767)
Great Creole food in this small, intimate restaurant. Lunch served from 12.30pm, dinner reservations necessary.

Coal Pot Restaurant $$$ ***
Vigie Marina
(☎ 452-5566)
Waterside dining in a wood and stone open- air structure, great atmosphere, Mediterranean, seafood and meat specialities.

Froggie Jacques $$-$$$
Vigie Bay
(☎ 458-1900)
A tropical bistro specialising in fish and seafood dishes set in a tranquil garden overlooking the Vigie Marina. Open for lunch and dinner Monday to Saturday. Reservations recommended.

EATING OUT IN CASTRIES

Green Parrot $$-$$$ ***
Old Morne Road
(☎ 452-3399)
Fabulous views over Castries with an excellent, large fixed price menu offering speciality local dishes using the best local ingredients from land and sea, great fun any night of the week.

KFC $ *
Bridge Street
(☎ 452-6444)
Fast food serving original, hot and spicy, crispy chicken, fries, soft drinks.

Kimlan's $-$$ ***
Micoud Street
(☎ 452-1136)
Offers good West Indian and Creole dishes and many specialities such as rotis, curries and stews.

La Bastide
La Clery
(☎ 452-2267)
An exquisite French restaurant just a 5-minute drive from Castries. Open for lunch Tuesday to Sunday. Permanent art exhibition.

Mandolin $$-$$$$**
Cara Suites
(☎ 452-4767)
A blend of modern British and classical French. Very good food and great views.

Paradise Pizza
14 Mary Ann Street
(☎ 451-7999)

Pasta and Pastry
Castries
(☎ 452-7196)
Italian food.

Restaurante de Romantique
$$-$$$ **
9 Mary Ann Street
(☎ 451-8790)
Romantic gourmet

Above: The Franco/St Lucian
Institute near Pointe Seraphine

Right: A cruise ship docked
alongside the Pointe Seraphine
Shopping Centre

Below: The lookout at the side of
the road on the Morne affords
an aerial view of Castries

SHOPPING

Shops are usually open 8.30am-12.30pm and 1.30-4pm Monday to Friday, and 8am-12noon on Saturday. The **Castries Market** is an excellent place to shop, especially if you are prepared to get up early although fruit, vegetables, spices and local handicrafts are sold all day.

At the cruiser terminal at **Pointe Seraphine**, there are a number of elegant boutiques in a Spanish-style shopping centre, offering Colombian emeralds, jewellery, cosmetics, perfumes and clothing. Closer to town is **La Place Carenage** on the waterfront which also offers duty free shopping but you must have your passport or airline ticket to buy. There is a new walk in Animation Cerre, describing the islands heritage with displays of arts and crafts which are also for sale. **Gablewood Mall** is open between 9am-9pm Monday to Saturday but some shops do stay open later, and the **Rodney Bay Marina Shopping Mall** has a wide selection of shops and restaurants. Most hotels also have their own shops and boutiques, many have an area set aside for vendors to sell local handicrafts.

Best buys are wood sculptures and carvings from **Vincent Eudovic's Studio** at Goodlands, outside Castries, batik, perfume, straw goods, pottery, silk screen goods, shell jewellery and leather goods.

Castries Market

The northern shore of the peninsula has miles of golden beaches, and the western tip contains a number of historic buildings and ruins. There are excellent views along the coast north and south by the Vigie Lighthouse, close by are the ruins of military buildings, a small powder magazine built by the French in 1784 and the graves of troops who died there.

The terminal is on the southern shore of the **Vigie Peninsula**, which forms the northern side of Castries Harbour and is home of Vigie Airport. Vigie appropriately is a French nautical term for a 'look-out'. Islanders will tell you that, not that long ago, motor traffic had to be halted when a plane was about to land or take off. Today the runway does not interfere with traffic, and there can be few airports in the world where you can step out of the terminal building, recently doubled in size, cross the road and be on the beach.

There are a couple of restaurants by the harbourside just south of the airport. Alternatively you can have a snack or drink at the terminal, and if the walk back to town seems daunting, take one of the many taxis that ply there.

Other places to visit in Castries include the area around the **Holy Trinity Church** off Trinity Church Road, to the north-west of the new market. Apart from the church there is the Anglican school and rectory, and to the north the **King George V Gardens**. The area also has a number of community buildings such as the headquarters of St John's Ambulance, Save the Children Fund and Girl Guides.

The area at the southern end of **Chaussee Road** is also worth visiting because it has a number of fine old creole houses with overhanging balconies and ornately patterned eaves.

For a fun boat trip out of Castries, take the brig *Unicorn*, a replica of a 19th Century square-rigged sailing ship. It offers fabulous views of the Pitons from the sea. The brig featured in the TV series *Roots*.

Also worth visiting is the Folk Research Centre, housed in a 19th Century colonial building on Mount Pleasant, just outside Castries. It catalogues every aspect of the island's cultural heritage from history, dance, music and folklore, all documented in the exhibition hall. ☎ 453-1477

A Circular Tour
Covering The South Of The Island

Driving west out of Castries and following the southern shores of the harbour leads you to **Tapion Bay** and then **La Toc Bay**, both popular hotel and resort areas.

South from Castries

If you head south out of Castries you have to climb over the **Morne Fortune**. There are several hairpin bends on the road, and you must observe the 'halt' signs on some corners if you are ascending. Stop on the white lines on the road because vehicles coming down the hill have to swing out into your path in order to negotiate the very tight bends. Listen out for approaching vehicles which usually toot their horns.

As you snake up the road that climbs the mountain, it is easy to appreciate its strategic importance. It commands spectacular views over Castries and the harbour, far out to sea and north along the coast to Pigeon Point.

The Morne

Because of its strategic importance, **the Morne** was constantly fought over by the English and French. The French started work on fortifying the Morne in the mid-eighteenth century and both countries, when in possession, continued this work. The restored **Fort Charlotte** near the summit, dates from the late 18th century and now houses a community college. The last positions were built by the English in 1905.

The most famous battle on Morne Fortune, however, was fought on 24 May 1796, when the Royal Inniskillin Fusiliers captured it from the French. A monument to their valour and victory still stands.

Some of the military buildings have been restored and are now used as an educational complex. The whole of the summit is a listed historic area. It is a fascinating place to wander around, as much of the original fortification still exists and there are several gun emplacements and cannon. Above all, however, you should visit the summit for the views which, in every direction, are stunning.

GETTING AROUND ST LUCIA

Car or jeep hire is the best option if you are planning to spend several days on the island and want to explore. If you want to plan only an occasional trip, use taxis or the island's 'bus' service. All towns and villages are connected to the main highways, and even though these side roads may be rough and pot holed, they are usually passable with care. However your insurance may not cover these roads.

Taxis are cheap and plentiful and can be ordered by telephone from your hotel, picked up at taxi ranks, at the airport, in Castries along Bridge Street and near the market. All taxi drivers have to attend special courses and they make excellent guides. Taxis can be hired by the trip, the hour or day for sightseeing tours, but make sure the price is agreed first, and you know which currency you are paying in. A taxi for up to four people to Castries from Hewanorra EC$125 (US$45), and from Castries to Rodney Bay EC$40 (US$15). Expect to pay EC$53 (US$20) an hour to hire a taxi, EC$318 (US$118) for an island tour and EC$250 (US$93) for a round trip taking in Soufrière and the sulphur springs.

Mini-buses, privately owned Japanese vans, ply the main routes on the island, generally carrying up to ten passengers. They offer an excellent way of getting around, provided you know where they are going, and they offer a great way of getting to know the islanders. Always check that the bus is heading in your direction before getting on. Most drivers have adopted flambouyant names which are boldly printed across the front of the vehicle, and music is generally played at near deafening volumes inside.

There are frequent minibus services between Castries and Gros Islet in the north of the island which run from early morning up to 10pm at night, and later on Fridays when the weekly 'jump up' takes place at Gros Islet. Services to the south are less frequent. There are services between Vieux Fort and Castries until early evening, but the last bus back from Soufrière

Marigot harbour, popularly known as Dolittle Bay

to Castries leaves around 12noon during the week, and around 3pm on Saturday. There is no scheduled bus service, and you just have to be patient until the next one comes along. Typical fares are EC$2 from Castries to Gros Islet, and EC$6 from Castries to Vieux Fort at the southern tip of the island.

There are boat services between Castries and Soufrière and these offer the most stunning views of the Pitons, and many hotels also run their own boats.

Helicopter transfers are available between Hewanorra and Castries, with helicopter pads additionally at Windjammer Landing, Jalousie Plantation, Pointe Seraphine and Rodney Bay.

You can charter your own plane, Helenair flies 15-seater Beachcraft 99 and 9 seater Britain Norman Islander aircraft around the Caribbean and is available for charter for trips, tours and aerial photography.

There are a number of studios in the area which are worth visiting, particularly **Bagshaw Studios** (head for La Toc and follow the signs) where you can watch silk screens being created.Open: Monday to Saturday 8.30am-4.30pm and Sunday 8.30am-1pm. Look out for the entrance as you climb up the hill, and further on, take Old Victorian Road, to visit **Caribelle Batik**, where silk and cotton batik are produced in the centuries old way. Open: Monday to Friday 8.30am-6pm and Saturday 8.30am-12.30pm.

Government House, the official residence of the Governor General, stands on the Morne and is a fine example of red-bricked late Victorian architecture. There is a museum and interpretation center although you must call first to make an appointment.

From the Morne, the road runs south into the Cul de Sac valley, a rich agricultural area with thousands of acres of bananas, formerly sugar cane, and an oil transhipment depot on the point north of where the Cul de Sac river runs into the sea. The banana freighters still call regularly to pick up bananas destined for the UK.

The island's only road tunnel is found on this stretch of road. It runs around Morne Fortune connecting the La Toc Road and Cul de Sac Valley. It cost $60m and was opened in Febuary 2000.

VINCENT EUDOVIC

As you start to descend into the valley, visit the studios of Vincent Eudovic, one of the island's most famous and talented sculptors.

Born at Babonneau on 15 April 1942, he attended Gros Islet primary school, and started sculpting at an early age. He first exhibited at the age of 12, and his sculpture 'Ali Baba' won first prize. After leaving school he moved to Trinidad and became a protege of Ricardo Vincente, under whom he studied for ten years. On his return to St Lucia he was employed by the Government to teach art, but he still felt he had more to learn, and with a UN scholarship, he went to Nigeria which proved a turning point. He first studied monumental sculpture working on pieces 20ft (6m) high, but then studied the traditional art of the Yoruba, especially the elaborate symbolism.

On his return to St Lucia, Eudovic taught for a time before opening his own gallery and workshop at Goodlands. He now holds about three exhibitions a year using local woods for his abstract carvings. The main wood used is **Laurier Canelle** which is now extinct, but he uses old stumps and uncovered roots found deep in the forest. He and fellow artists also use mahogany, teak, Laurier Mabouey, and red and white cedar.

He has won many international awards and his works have been displayed and exhibited in many countries.

Eudovic's Art Studio also operates a small guest-house and restaurant which offers fabulous views over the lush valley below. Mr Eudovic is now producing small sculptures in Laurier Canelle of a convenient size to take home. The studio is open Monday to Saturday from 8.30am-5 or 6pm, Sundays in winter.

TOWARDS MARIGOT BAY

From Cul de Sac valley, the windy, hilly road then runs south towards **Marigot Bay**. You have to turn off to visit the bay, but it is well worth the detour, and the road literally ends at the water's edge beside a police and customs station which must have one of the best locations in the world. You can get a mini-bus from Castries to get to the bay but it will probably drop you off at the main road and you will have to walk the last mile or so down to the water — and walk back for the return journey to Castries.

Marigot Bay, one of the most beautiful anchorages in the Caribbean was the setting of the film Doctor Dolittle, starring Rex Harrison, and scenes from Sophia Loren's Fire Power were also filmed here. Yachts bob up and down in the turquoise waters, and the bay is surrounded on three sides by lush foliage covered hills which slope down to the water's edge decorated with palm trees.

Admiral Barrington is said to have evaded a French naval force in 1778 by sailing his squadron into the bay and camouflaging the vessels with palm leaves.

A free ferry plies across to **Dolittles** with its water-side restaurant, and it is a delightful place for a beach lunch before continuing with your explorations. There are usually lots of boats anchored or moving about in the bay, with dinghies coming ashore. There are also some good restaurants on the road side of the bay, and, you can normally watch islanders crafting hats and baskets from woven banana leaves, which are sold along with other handicrafts and souvenirs by the water.

Just three minutes inland from Marigot Bay in the Roseau Valley is the island's only rum distillery. Enjoy a tour and sampling ☎ 451-4258.

FROM MARIGOT BAY

From Marigot Bay, the road continues south through the Roseau Banana Plantation and the small fishing village of **Massacré** with its community housing project, to **Anse La Raye** with its imposing church,

and **Canaries**. Both villages nestle in their own small bay fed by a river, and backed by steeply rising hills, and depend largely on the sea for their livelihood.

Every Friday, Anse La Raye holds a seafood 'jump up', a very lively and flavorsome evening.

Just before the bridge in Anse La Raye is a crossroads and a small sign to the **La Sikwi Historical Mill and Plantation** to the left. Turn for this, bearing right at a Y junction. Stop at the new footbridge over the river (replacing one of many destroyed in the September 1994 flood). The

---

The Invergoll Estate

The Invergoll Estate is 120 years old and extends to 400 acres (160 hectares). It used to produce sugar but changed to citrus juice during the 1940s. It now produces bananas, cocoa and a little coffee. The tour includes the old sugar mill (La Sikwi) with its 40ft (12m) overshot waterwheel fed by an aquaduct. The wheel dates from 1878 and was made in Glasgow, Scotland. Note the milling machinery made by Fletchers of Derby, England. They provided virtually all sugar milling equipment to the world before the industry collapsed.

There is a restaurant and bar here and a theatre set in the botanical garden. It hosts a jazz festival but mostly features local folk music bi-monthly. There are also tours to the Anse La Raye waterfalls and rain forest. If you wish to book through your hotel you may, or alternatively Carib Touring can organise things for you (☎ 452 1141).

The marina at Marigot harbour

bridge gives access to the 400-acre estate with its museum, cultural theater and 40 foot water wheel set in lovely gardens.

As you drive along the new road between Anse La Raye and Canaries, you get your first good view of the **Pitons** (spikes) across Soufrière Bay. These huge natural pyramids rise from the sea, and from a distance seem to be side by side. It is only as you travel inland between them, that you can appreciate just how far apart they are. **Petit Piton** is the nearer of the two, with **Gros Piton** almost 1¹/₂ miles (2km) beyond across Anse des Pitons.

The road hugs the western flanks of the mountain which rise up into a vast area of rain forest. You can only visit the forest, now a protected area, with a guide but it is worth the visit, and makes a fascinating and unforgettable day trip.

The road then starts to descend from the mountains towards the coast. Before heading into Soufrière it is worth making a detour up the very bumpy road that leads to the **Anse Chastanet Resort**. It is said the road is not repaired to discourage too many visitors, but it is worth taking because as it climbs up the hill there are stunning views of the Pitons behind you. From across the water you can take excellent photographs of the two mountains clearly separated by the sea.

Just south of Castries is Anse La Liberte camping and heritage site. It is the islands only camping site and spreads well over 133 acres. There is a small beach, hiking trails and a wealth of plant and bird life.

Bon Appetit $$ ***
Morne Fortune
(☎ 452-2757)
Worth it for the scenic views over
Castries, but even more so for the
intimate atmosphere, attentive,
personal service and great food.
There are only five tables so book for
dinner. The restaurant is run by
Renato and Cheryl Venturi. All soups
and starters are home made, and the
house speciality is freshwater
crayfish. You can also enjoy great fish
and steaks.

Chateau My'Go
Marigot Bay
(☎ 451-4772)
Eat on an open-air upstairs balcony
overlooking the bay or in the cool,
tropical garden. Enjoy home grown
vegetables and family recipes
handed down through the years.
East Indian and Creole style meals.

Dolittles $-$$
(☎ 451-4974)
Reached by water taxi on the north
side of the bay.
Sample Caribbean and continental
fare or sip a cocktail while watching
yachts cruise by on sparkling,
turquoise water.

Eudovic's $$ **
Goodlands
(☎ 452-2747)
A fabulous setting perched on the hill
and looking out over great scenery.
The restaurant is owned by one of the
island's most famous sculptors and

you dine surrounded by many of his
hand carvings. You can buy them
afterwards.

JJ's Paradise Restaurant & Bar
$-$$ **
Marigot Bay
(☎ 451-4076)
West Indian, French and local
speciality dishes are served in the
restaurant which is a leisurely ten
minute walk from the bay. There is
even free transport for those who
can't face the walk. Open from
7.30pm until the last guests leave.
There is a great party atmosphere on
Friday nights when JJ's throws its
weekly jam.

Kimono's $$$ **
Sandals St Lucia,
La Toc Bay
(☎ 452-3081)
This popular restaurant serves
exotic oriental cuisine in a theatrical
Teppanyaki setting. There is a no-
smoking rule at Kimono's and the
dress code is casually elegant.
Reservations are required.

Los Pitons $-$$ **
Sandals St Lucia,
La Toc Bay
(☎ 452-3081)
Specialising in Caribbean cuisine the
Pitons is open for West Indian
dinner every night of the week. The
restaurant also opens for breakfast
and lunch every day except
Mondays. The dress code is casually
elegant.

Oceana
La Toc Road
Next to sandals
(☎ 456-0300)
A seafood restaurant with a
relaxed atmosphere. The menu
included Scotch Bonnet Crusted
Snapper and Shrimp Copacabana.
Open for lunch 12 noon to 2.30
and dinner 6pm to 11pm.

The Pavilion $$-$$$ ***
Sandals St Lucia,
La Toc Bay
(☎ 452-3081)
The resort's main dining area situated
by the pool and delightful for dinner
in the evening. The cuisine is a mix of
international with strong Italian
influences. A beach barbecue is held
weekly, two nights feature an Italian
buffet, and there is an international
buffet weekly. Breakfast is served
daily from 7.30-10.15am, lunch from
12.30-2.15pm and dinner between
6.30-10.15pm. Reservations
required.

Rainforest Hideaway
Marigot Bay
(☎ 286-0511)
St. Lucia's newest fine restaurant
serves a fusion of Asian, Oriental
and Caribbean dishes. The dinner
menu changes daily reflecting
seasonal ingredients. Dine on the
dock surrounded by a lush, tropical
landscape. Enjoy the champagne
bar and live jazz bands.
Open for lunch and dinner six days
a week. Reservations
recommended. Ferry fares
refunded.

Restaurant La Toc $$$ ***
Sandals St Lucia,
La Toc Bay
(☎ 452-3081)
Authentic French Restaurant
featuring fine European dining and
white glove service. Open for
dinner every night. Dress code is
formal. Reservations required.

Tapion Reef Hotel $$-$$$ **
Tapion Bay
(☎ 452-7471)
The restaurant has a good a la carte
menu featuring West Indian and
Creole dishes. Noted for its seafood
and freshwater crayfish. The
restaurant and bar overlook historic
Tapion Rock. Dinner reservations
recommended.

Above: The restaurant at Marigot harbour
Below: The beach at Anse La Raye

Above: Sandals La Toc

Below: The banana plantation at Cul de Sac Valley

SOUFRIÈRE

Even though it no longer enjoys the prosperity of a century or so ago, when it was a busy port, Soufrière is still a wonderfully picturesque fishing town. It nestles in the shadows of the Pitons, with Soufrière Bay to the west and the sulphur gushing volcanic crater which gives it its name, just inland to the south-east.

HISTORY

Although the French established the first permanent settlement in the latter half of the seventeenth century, there is lots of evidence that early Amerindian settlers had lived here before this. There are many petroglyphs (**rock paint-ings**) in the area, particularly at Stonefields, and the rock terraces at Belfond are believed to be their work.

The French established huge plantations by clearing the grounds of trees and scrub, and slaves were shipped from Africa to man them. In 1746 Soufrière became the first town of St Lucia. It has been an important trading and farming centre ever since.

By 1775 there were more than 100 estates around the

Revolutionary Soufrière

Soufrière had only just started to recover from the hurricane of 1780 when it was hit again by the effects of the **French Revolution** of 1789. The Revolutionary council in Paris ordered that all French names on the island be changed, and Soufrière was renamed La Convention. A **guillotine** was even erected in the Town Square for a time, and some of the Royalist planters were taken prisoner and lost their heads, while the others fled.

It was a time of great turmoil on the island, especially around the town. Slaves who had been freed by order of Paris joined forces with French soldiers who had deserted because of atrocious living conditions and poor or no pay. Between 1794 and 1797, the time of the **Brigand Wars**, these bands lived in the hills and made frequent raids to the coast, wrecking almost everything in their path. Nearly all the buildings rebuilt after the hurricane were destroyed.

---

town, most producing sugar or coffee, and with names such as Diamond, Ruby and La Perle. Soufrière at this time had a population of around 2,000 and was regarded as 'the bread basket of St Lucia'.

Soufrière was particularly badly hit in 1780 by one of the worst hurricanes ever to hit the Windwards Islands.

When stability returned to the island, at the end of the Brigand Wars, the town resumed its original name of Soufrière, its buildings were rebuilt, and many of the estates in the area brought back into production.

St Lucia was finally granted to Britain by the **Treaty of Paris** in 1814 and in 1838 all slaves on the island were given their freedom. Although they could now legally own land, most chose to remain on the estates as paid workers, and many of the town's present population are directly descended from the early French plantation owners or their slaves.

The town's strong French heritage can still be seen and heard. Many family names are of French origin, as are many of the places and geographical features nearby — Anse Mamin, Etangs, Fond St Jacques, Terre Blanche and Malgre Tout for instance.

The town has been hit by four major disasters in the last 200 years. In 1839 the church was seriously damaged by an **earthquake**, in 1955 half the town was destroyed by a **huge fire** which burned all night, and in 1980 **Hurricane Allen** slammed ashore. While the town escaped serious damage, roads to and from were blocked by landslides and large areas of the rainforest inland were torn apart. On 10 September 1994 the area was hit by a ferocious **storm** that caused the worst flooding for 75 years. In $3\frac{1}{2}$ hours, 11 inches (28cm) of rain fell. Rivers flooded washing away homes and bridges, and massive landslides destroyed months of work on new projects such as the new Castries to Soufrière road. Although it was the worst storm in living memory, only six people lost their lives.

SOUFRIÈRE TODAY

Today, the town has a remarkably peaceful aspect whether approaching by land or sea. Soufrière Bay offers a sheltered anchorage for yachts, and the dock which juts out into the water accommodates boats

Josephine

Soufrière is also noted as the home of Marie-Josephe-Rose de Tascher de la Pagerie, better known as **Empress Josephine**, wife of Napoleon Bonaparte. Although born at Morne Paix Bouche in the north of St Lucia, she spent much of her childhood at **Mal Maison**, her father's estate on the outskirts of Soufrière. The estate can still be visited and much of it must still look as it did when she stayed there. There is still the massive iron water wheel used to power the rollers which crushed the sugar cane, and the iron crucibles in which the sugar was boiled. There is also the copper press where oil was extracted from limes, and the copra sheds where cocunuts were cut in half and laid out to dry. Women can still be seen husking the coconuts ready for drying, and removing beans from the cocoa pods.

Soufrière's location is stunning and there are many places of natural and historic interest to visit in the area, both inland and offshore. The drive back from Soufrière to Castries takes about one hour.

offering sightseeing trips and trips to and from Castries, such as the impressive brig *Unicorn*.

The long stretch of sandy beach is lined with coconut palms, beneath which lie the open fishing boats after a day at sea. The waterfront is a bustling place in the afternoon when the boats have returned as the fishermen sell their catches, and people from surrounding villages bring their produce for sale at the Saturday market.

The **Soufrière River** splits the town in two and most of the shops, craft centres, restaurants and guest houses are found in the two or three streets inland from the jetty, including the police station and post office. Many of the houses along the waterfront have been restored, and many of the buildings have a special charm with old stone frontages, and there are many traditional creole homes with ornate filigree friezes beneath their corrugated iron roofs.

The town was used as the location for the film *Water*, filmed in 1984 and starring Michael Caine.

The Caribbean Giclee gallery in the old courthouse features the work of many artists from St Lucia as well as those who visit the island to paint.

Above: Soufrière Jetty and Petit Piton

Below: Ornate filigree friezes on traditional creole homes, Soufrière

ANSE CHASTANET

Just to the north at **Anse Chastanet**, a reef rich in marine life lies just off the beach, it is a designated Marine National Park. Divers claim it is one of the most beautiful reefs in the region because of its multi-coloured corals, sponges and shoals of tropical fish. It is an area rich in brain coral, sea fans and vase sponges. Species of fish include angel fish, sargeant majors, squirrel fish, grunts, blue-headed wrasse, doctor fish, the solitary parrot fish and flying gurnards.

The **Anse Chastanet Hotel** is a delightful forty-nine room hotel situated on a lush 600-acre (240 hectare) estate. Guests are welcomed by charming staff and are accommodated in unique and stylish rooms. The bedrooms, bathrooms and tropical hardwood furniture have been personally designed by nick Troubetzksy the architect-owner and all blend delightfully with the surrounding environment. The furniture has been handmade in the region using many of the island woods including teak, mahogany, red cedar and wild breadfruit.

The owner first arrived in St Lucia in 1970 and stayed on to transform Anse Chastanet into the peaceful haven it has become (no TV room, telephones or radios). With his wife Karolin, they run the hotel in a most hospitable and elegant fashion. There is a spa and art gallery.

Thirty-six open treehouse-style deluxe rooms are situated on a hillside adorned with spectacular flowering trees and twelve rooms are situated directly on the beach, just steps from the water's edge. Guests are welcomed into a charming and romantic property which provides a true escape from the outside world. Days are spent lazing on the tropical beaches or enjoying the underwater splendour of the coral reefs. just feet from the beach

The hotel offers complimentary snorkelling, windsurfing, sailing and tennis. It has the largest dive center on the island and is developing its second beach Las Anse Mamin. St Lucia's landmark adventure destination offering jungle biking, nature and hiking trails, rock climbing, scuba, snorkelling and watersports.

Leave behind the cares of the world and enjoy candlelit dinners in either the open-air restaurant located in the shadow of the magnificent sugar-loafed peaks of the Pitons, or in the enchanting Trou au Diable restaurant situated right on the sandy beach. The cuisine is fresh and delicious and utilizes local specialities including seafood served in a mouth-watering Creole-style sauce.

SOUFRIÈRE VOLCANO

The road south of town leads to St Lucia's drive-in volcano, the **Soufrière volcano**. The giant crater was formed during a period of massive volcanic activity about 40,000 years ago.

Well trained guides explain the geological history of the area and how the moonscape-like landscape was created. There are up to 24 cauldrons of bubbling mud boiling at around 340°F (171°C) over 7 acres (3 hectares). The area is filled with steam and smell of sulphur. The last volcanic activity occurred between 1760 and 1780 although it was not significant. The volcano is still monitored closely although it is regarded as dormant because most of the subterranean pressure has been released.

During the oil crisis in the 1970s an attempt was made to harness the boiling thermal waters so they could drive turbines. The scheme failed because the viscous lava was so acidic that it corroded the drilling pipes and well head caps.

As you overlook the bubbling mud pools, you can see just how vast the crater is as the surrounding mountains mark out the original 12km diameter of the volcano. The eruption was so massive that it blew the centre of the volcano apart and most of this finished up in the sea to the west. Large areas of the crater are covered with vegetation and it is amazing that sixty people actually live within the perimeter of the crater earning their living either farming or selling souvenirs to visitors.

Don't stray from the designated paths as the area around the boiling mud pools is very dangerous. A few years ago, an unqualified guide was demonstrating just how soft the ground was by jumping up and down on it. Suddenly the ground caved in, the guide was badly burned and the hole is now the largest cauldron on the acre-large hot site.

Above: The "drive in volcano", south-east of Soufrière

Left: The Diamond Waterfall close to the Mineral Baths

Below: The Diamond Estate Botanical Garden

THE ST LUCIA NATIONAL TRUST

The St Lucia National Trust was established in 1975 and is run by a Council of voluntary members. All revenues are used towards the conservation of the island's heritage, and the Trust is supported by the Government of St Lucia and voluntary contributions.

The Trust cooperates with the Ministry of Planning over matters of conservation, as well as several other Government departments and interested bodies, at national, regional and international level. Substantial assistance for the Pigeon Island project came from: the British Development Division in the UK, the Canadian International Development Agency, Organisation of American States and Rodney Bay Ltd in St Lucia. Assistance for the new Museum came from: the Small Project Implementation Facility in Canada, the Canadian and St Lucian Governments and Canadian and St Lucian architects, consultants and contractors.

DIAMOND ESTATE

There are also sulphur springs on the Diamond Estate which was founded in 1784 for the troops of King Louis XVI of France so that they could benefit from the therapeutic waters. **Baron de Micoud,** Governor of St Lucia at the time, sent samples from the hot springs to France for analysis by the Médicin du Roi. They found that the waters contained the same healing powers as the spa at Aix-les-Bains in France and Aix-la-Chapelle (Aachen) in Germany.

The King was so impressed that he made available the necessary funds to construct the main building and about twelve stone baths. The catchment built then to feed the baths is still used today. The baths were only used for about eight years until the French Revolution. Unfortunately the bath house was totally destroyed during the Brigand War. The baths themselves fell into disrepair and

79

were eventually covered by plants and undergrowth.

It was not until 1930 that Andre Du Boulay, owner of the Soufrière and Diamond Estate decided to excavate and restore two baths for his own use. Later the outside pools were built and opened to the public for a small fee. The heated mineral-rich waters are said to cure a number of ailments and you can bathe in the waters for a small charge. There are changing cubicles close at hand.

The Estate was already well established with citrus trees and cocoa, and in 1983 after the death of M. Du Boulay, his daughter Joan Devaux took over control of both Soufrière and Diamond. She determined to landscape the natural gorge, which is the main feature of Diamond, as an historical garden. Today, it is a blaze of colour with hibiscus, ixora, heliconias and glorious Balisier and scores of other plants and trees. There are rare orchids including the vanilla, which only bears its aromatic pods after every flower has been hand pollinated.

Apart from the original coconut and cocoa trees, there are nutmeg, citrus, mango and yland ylang trees. Ornamental palms include golden stem, fan palm and merrils palm. There are Norfolk pine and Casuarina conifers, and luxuriant shrubs and ground hugging flowers. Anthurium is one of the garden's most dramatic flowers with its blood red, heart-shaped bract. Other flowering plants include the purple heliconia, also known as wild banana, which acts as a magnet for humming birds, the sun loving hibiscus, exotic frangipani, and stunning yellow allamanda.

The gardens are beautifully maintained and landscaped with pergolas, gazebos, rockeries and arbours. Name labels allow you to identify the various plants, and there are several displays showing how various fruits and plants look after their shells or outer casings have been removed.

The path leads you to the two outdoor **Diamond Mineral Baths** and changing huts, and then continues along a fern-lined walk to a glade with its waterfall which tumbles into a rock pool. The water, which comes straight from the volcano crater, is so mineral-laden that it has stained the rocks behind the waterfall a bright orange colour. The water is more than 100°F (37°C) when it leaves the crater on its descent to the waterfall.

The gardens are open daily from 10am to 5pm and Sunday 10am to 3pm. For more information contact the Diamond Botanical Gardens, Diamond Estate, PO Box 1020, Castries ☎ 459-7565.

Soufrière Estate

The **Soufrière Estate** was originally part of a 2,000 acre (800 hectare) land grant by King Louis XIV in 1713 to three Devaux brothers from Normandy. The brothers arrived in St Lucia in 1742 to establish their plantations, and the family still owns them today. The brothers escaped the guillotine because they were hidden by faithful slaves.

The Baron de Micoud, who later took over the estate, was killed in a duel so the church refused to let him be buried on sanctified ground. Instead he was buried on the estate. The young Empress Josephine played with the Devaux children at the Soufrière Estate, which was close to her father's Mal Maison Plantation which is open daily 10am-4pm. The plantation can be visited

and tours offer a fascinating insight into the harvesting and processing of crops such as copra and cocoa.

You can also tour the mini-zoo with local animals such as agouti, manicou and boa constrictors and see one of the oldest and most impressive water wheels still operating in the Caribbean. It was imported early in the 19th century to crush sugar cane, then used to crush limes and more recently, supplied electricty to Soufrière.

Morne Coubaril Estate

Another estate, open daily 9am-5pm, which has opened its gates to visitors is **Morne Coubaril Estate**. It has always had a French owner and has views down onto the town of Soufrière. In fact it was fortified by the French to protect the bay and one of the old guns survives. It is about 1 mile (2km) out of town on the road to Choiseul.

This is a working estate and the guide shows you around the copra oven for reducing coconuts, the cocoa processing house, the manioc house and recreated houses of the Carib Indians and African slaves ☎ 459-7340.

Top: The manioc house, on the Morne Coubaril Estate

Above: Typical rain forest viewed from the west coast road

Left: Gros Piton and Anse des Pitons

Opposite page: The Still Restaurant, near Soufrière

Almost opposite the Morne Coubaril gates is the drive to **Jalousie Hilton Plantation Resort** and spa, one of the most exclusive resorts on the island. It offers all the facilities of a top class resort, excellent food and one of the most stunning beaches in the world. The resort is situated between the two Pitons and Petit Piton rises as a sheer wall some 1,000ft (305m) from the beach.

Apart from driving tours around Soufrière, many companies offer full day boat trips from Castries and the resort areas. You not only get the chance to visit this interesting area, you can enjoy a cruise down the island's beautiful west coast as well. Also worth visiting is the **Fond Doux Estate**, a 250 year old working estate with spectacular views, historical remains, crops and wildlife ☎ 459-7545.

INLAND FROM SOUFRIÈRE

Inland from Soufrière, the road climbs steeply through dense, lush vegetation into one of the island's few remaining areas of tropical rain forest. About 11 per cent of the island is covered by rain forest while in the seventeenth century all of it was.

At 3,118 feet (945m), Mount Gimie is the highest point in St. Lucia and there are guided tours up the mountain through dense rain forests. It is worth the hike for the wildlife and the moment when you climb above the tree line and have most of the island spread out below you.

There are spectacular views from the rough **Fond St Jacques** road back over the Pitons and Soufrière, and the forests themselves are home to hundreds of exotic birds, animals, plants and insects. The forest is home to the vivid orange Flambeau butterfly, the St Lucia Oriole, St Lucia Forest Thrush and St Lucia Blackfinch, all only found on the island. There are flycatchers, bananaquits, birds of prey and tiny humming birds, and, if you are really

Anse Chastanet Hotel $-$$ **
Anse Chastanet
(☎ 459-7000)
The beach restaurant and bar offers freshly cooked food and a good value, varied menu, while the Piton Restaurant perches on a cliff 100ft (30m) above the sea, and looks out over the beach and Caribbean. The restaurant's set five course menu offers a good choice, and is excellent value for money.

Archies's
Bridge Street
Soufriere
(☎ 459-7760)
Small friendly restaurant specialising in local cuisine. Vegetarian and Indian dishes.

Dasheene $$-$$$ ***
Ladera Resort
(☎ 459-7323)
Exciting food combining new wave Californian and traditional

Caribbean, with fresh produce and culinary fare combining to create some memorable dishes. One of the best restaurants on the island and an impressive wine list, and an even more impressive view as the restaurant is perched 1,000ft (305m) up on the mountainside. Open daily.

Fond Deux Estate
Near Soufriere
(☎ 459-7545)
Located at the 250 year old Estate near Soufriere. Creole and European style meals served in a setting of tropical flowers and lush forest trees.

The Humming Bird $-$$ **
Beach Resort
(☎ 459-7232)
The waterside restaurant serves great seafood, always fresh and prepared to order. Try the crayfish, lobster, king crab or octopus. There are great vief the Pitons and a pool to cool off in.

lucky, you might catch sight of the rare and colourful St Lucia parrot, one of the world's most endang-ered species, and the island's national bird.

Thanks to careful management and habitat conservation, the St Lucia parrot population once down to less than a 100, is now back to 200 and still growing. It is most likely to be spotted early in the morning or late in the afternoon as it flies to its feeding areas. If you don't actually see it, you cannot mistake its raucous cries as it flies through the trees.

Look out for lizards scurrying around on the forest floor and the lumbering Goliath

Jalousie Hillon $$-$$$ ***
Near Soufrière
(☎ 459-8000)
There are four restaurants in this luxury resort just up the coast from Soufrière. The Verandah offers breakfast, the Pier specialises in seafood and Creole dishes. The Plantation Room offers fine dining with foods from the Mediterranean fused with Eastern Cuisine.

La Haut Plantation $$-$$$
(☎ 459-7008)
Excellent views, great service and good food. Open daily for breakfast, lunch and Dinner. Reservations recommended. Excellent Caribbean cuisine. Everything's good but try the creamy clam chowder, curry goat and jerk pork.

Mago Estate Restaurant $$
(☎ 459-5880)
Set on a hill just outside Soufriere and over looking the Pitons. Open air all day dining.

The Old Courthouse Restaurant & Bar
(☎ 459-5002)
Located on the waterfront and specialising in French, Creole and South-East Asian dishes.

The Still $-$$ ***
La Perle and Ruby Estates
(☎ 459-7261)
A family owned restaurant offering genuine St Lucian dishes in a delightful plantation setting. There is also an impressive lunch buffet which offers the chance to taste a number of island specialities. Open daily from 8am to 5pm and for dinner by reservation only.

beetle. The foliage and scent is breathtaking, with giant tree ferns, bamboo stands, and giant gommier, mahogany and cedar trees, wild orchids and air plants clinging to the bark of their host trees.

Walks through the **Edmond Forest Reserve** can be arranged through tour guides, or through the Forestry and Lands Department in Castries. If you go on an organised tour, the bus will drop you at the edge of the rain forest, and your guide will escort you along a track through the dense undergrowth. The walking is not that strenuous but you should be reasonably fit and have good footwear.

Soufrière to Vieux Fort

From Soufrière the road climbs into the mountains and rain forests past the Pitons on your right, and then drops down to the coast. You can take one of the many side roads which lead to the coast and pass close by Gros Piton.

The Pitons

The two Pitons, **Gros Piton** to the south at 2,619ft (798m), and **Petit Piton** to the north at 2,461ft (750m), are giant volcanic plugs left behind as a result of volcanic activity long ago. They tower out of the sea, and both can be climbed but the ascent is rated difficult, and a full day is needed for the round trip. Guides are recommended.

Gros Piton

You can explore Gros Piton along a well marked nature trail. The trail starts at the fond

The Maria Islands near Vieux Fort

86

Gens Libre Community (village of the free people). It was first settled by runaway slaves during the 1748 rebellion. You can still see the caves and signal stations they created. The first half of the trail is 'moderate' while the second half is 'strenuous'. Allow at least 4 hours for the round trip and use a guide not just because the weather can change suddenly but also because of their local knowledge of the history, nature and folkelore of the area. Gros Piton Guides Association ☎ 459-9748.

A detour to **La Pointe** is worthwhile, if you take the road for La Pointe and L'Ivrogne, which follows the L'Ivrogne River, you can also take in the **Nature Trail** along the way. The gravel paved looped trail takes about an hour to walk. Most of the tree species — such as mahogany and Caribbean pine — are still used commercially on the island and they provide cover for many bird species, especially singing warblers, finches and hummingbirds. There are ground and tree lizards, a medicinal herb

garden and many of the fruit bearing trees that can be found throughout the island, and an interpretive centre with information about endangered species, vegetation zones and the rain forest by day and night.

The fishing village of **La Pointe** is also the centre of the island's pottery industry. Local clay is shaped into mainly functional domestic pots. There are the massive coal pots, traditional cooking pots, and canaries, another version of the cooking pot brought from Africa.

From La Pointe take the coastal road south rather than returning to the main highway.

CHOISEUL

Next is the tiny fishing village of **Choiseul** with its church almost on the beach, and Crafts Centre which is open Monday to Friday 8am-4pm and Saturday 10am-4pm. The village is noted for its weavers who work mostly with straw, kus-kus, vertiver grass and wicker. Again, they turn out mostly functional items such as baskets, mats, sewing boxes, fans and laundry baskets. At one time, almost all St Lucian babies slept in locally woven bassinets.

The **Craft Centre** has also been instrumental in improving the skills of local bamboo weavers. Traditional because of its strength, bamboo was used to weave large baskets and containers, mostly for agriculture and usually lacking much refinement. Now, after a six year training programme involving Taiwanese teachers, much more refined and elaborate products are being made. The village also has a flourishing furniture industry, producing mostly chairs from cedar, with screw pine fibre woven backs.

The Crafts Centre has a shop where you can buy locally made goods, and you can wander around the workshops watching the craftsmen and women at work. You can even arrange to spend a day doing pottery, basket weaving or wood carving under the watchful eye of **Marinus Francois**, the resident woodwork instructor, whose own creations are beautiful. The Crafts Centre is also putting together **day long craft tours** which allow you to see different artists at work — basket weavers at Morne Sion, pottery being produced at La Pointe and straw weavers at Mongouge.

Choiseul is a charming village with its old gingerbread houses on stilts overlooking

EATING OUT IN & AROUND VIEUX FORT

Inexpensive $ Moderate $$ *Expensive $$$*
The * system (from one to four) is based on quality of food, service and ambience.

Chak Chak Cafe $-$$ **
Vieux Fort
(☎ 454-6260)
Close to Hewanorra Airport and offering continental and Creole daily specials.

Golden Harvest Chinese Restaurant
New Dock Road
Vieux Fort
(☎ 454-6655)
Chinese Food.

Il Pirata Ristorante Italiano
$-$$ **
(☎ 454-6610)
An Italian restaurant on the beach, offering relaxed dining and authentic cuisine, with a good Italian wine list. Open daily except Monday from 7am-9.30pm.

Juliette's Lodge $$
Beanfield
(☎ 454-5300)
Good Creole, steaks and scampi.

The Reef Restaurant & Bar
$-$$ ***
Anse du Sables
(☎ 454-3418)
The cafe is on the beach and offers a wide range of Caribbean and international food, including some very good vegetarian dishes.

the bay, many of the properties having the ornate fretwork which is so typical of the island.

Balenbouche is one of the many hidden gems of St. Lucia. It is a former sugar plantation and although the old mills are now in ruins, you can still see the huge water wheel and the 18th century estate house that survive in charming grounds. Although a private property, you can visit with the owner's permission and can even dine

Choiseul village sits literally on the beach

and stay in the house or a cottage if you book in advance. ☎ 455-1244.

The road then follows the coast to **Laborie**, another beautiful little fishing village, and Vieux Fort at the southern end of the island. **Morne Le Blanc** rises behind laborie and you can see the island of St Vincent from the summit. Planes from around the world fly into **Hewanorra International Airport** which has recently undergone an extensive expansion with new lounges, restaurants, duty free shops and boutiques, and improvements to the runway and a walkway to the terminal building.

Vieux Fort

Vieux Fort commands views over a wide bay. It was named after a fortress which used to look out over St Vincent in the distance. In the second half of the 18th century it was the centre of the island's sugar industry, but its fortunes declined as the sugar cane plantations closed.

A new lease of life came during the Second World War when the Americans built an airstrip as a refuelling stop for planes flying between the US and Europe. The much expanded airstrip is now Hewanorra International Airport.

Island Windsurfing is based in Vieux Fort and operates in Anse Sables, and they hire equipment and give lessons. Their Reef Beach Cafe includes a video lounge where you can learn about the sport before getting your feet wet.

Just outside Vieux Fort are the **Mankote Mangrove Swamps,** the main source of nutrients for the island's natural fish nursery in nearby Savannes Bay. There is a view-ing tower. Guided tours can be arranged through the St Lucia National Trust ☎ 452-5005.

You can drive down to Ministre Point, the most southerly point on the island at the end of the **Moule a Chique Peninsula**. Apart from the lighthouse perched on the rocks and the incredible views across to St Vincent and the Grenadines, the cliffs are home to thousands of sea birds. If you look out to sea you can normally see where the cold dark blue waters of the Atlantic meet the warm turquoise waters of the Caribbean.

This whole area is a bird watcher's paradise. The two islands to the east off Vieux Fort — Maria Major and Maria Minor, make up the **Maria Islands Nature Reserve** which contains many rare species of plants and birds, including some not found elsewhere in the Caribbean. Maria Major is the only place in the world where the harmless kouwes grass snake is found, and the islands are also host to the unique Zandoli Te ground lizard. The male has a remarkable brilliant blue tail. The reserve is closed during the breeding season but tours can be arranged at other times.

Savannes Bay

VIEUX FORT TO CASTRIES ALONG THE EAST COAST

From Vieux Fort the new road follows the Atlantic coastline north past Savannes Bay and the Savannes Bay Nature Reserve and Point de Caille to Micaud. Along the way there are spectacular views along the rocky coastline, often pounded by Atlantic breakers. You will notice the difference between the sheltered western coast and the exposed Atlantic coast which almost always has an onshore breeze. When the breeze picks up, the waves come powering in which makes this a very popular area for experienced wind surfers and surf boarders.

There are many bays along this stretch of coastline such as Anse L'Islet, Anse Ger and Troumassé Bay. There are usually steep roads down to these coves, and the last section often has to be done on foot.

About a mile inland from Micoud between the villages of Praslin and Mon Repos are Mamiku Gardens the Latille Falls. The tropical gardens are a blaze of color with exotic fruits and flowers and a number of waterfalls ☎ 454-0202.

Between the two fishing villages of Micoud and Dennery,

and just after the small fishing village of Praslin, you can see the **Fregate Islands** just off shore. The tiny islands are the nesting site of frigate birds. Tours can be arranged through the St Lucia National Trust (☎ 25005/31495).

Continue to Praslin where fishermen still carve their canoes from gommier trees. Work has started here on a new resort complex that will feature 3 hotels and a marina.

Mamiku Gardens offers 12 acres of landscaped gardens and woodlands in the grounds of a 17th century estate house. Originally acquired in 1766 by Baron de Micoud, a French army colonel and former governor of the island, the estate gets its name from the Baron's wife. As she was Madame de Micoud, the locals referred to the property as Ma Micoud's estate, and this was eventually abbreviated to Mamiku. By the end of the 18th century, however, the estate house had become a British military post under the control of General Sir Jolin Moore. It saw a lot of action because of pirates and brigands and the house was eventually destroyed by fire after a battle that left 15 soldiers dead.

Today, the estate is a working plantation producing bananas, tropical fruits and flowers and has been run by the Shingleton-Smith family since 1906. The botanical gardens is the latest attraction and features endangered St. Lucian trees, Creole bush medicine garden, the estate house ruins. An ongoing archaeological dig has uncovered pieces of 18th century pottery. There is also a bar and gift shop.

Dennery is one of the most beautiful villages on the island and has a long tradition as both a fishing and boat building community. The fishing boats are all hand built and were traditionally made from trees felled in the rain forests. Efforts are being made with some success to encourage the' boat builders to use fibre glass in their construction to protect the trees.

Well worth visiting is another of the Heritage Tours Members, **Fond d'or** just north of Dennery. With the assistance of excellent guides you can retrace the island's past – from early Amerindian settlements to historic sugar plantation buildings. There are hiking and nature trails winding through tropical vegetation along the river out to a beautiful white sand beach. open daily ☎ 453-3242.

Just beyond Dennery the road turns inland and there is another opportunity to visit a working agricultural estate at the **Errard Plantation**, open daily. The plantation which specialises in bananas, runs either side of the Errard River. This is a private estate and it is best to seek permission before progressing along the rough road until you see the small **Errard Waterfall** which can be reached by a short trail. Better still, take one of the organised day trips to the estate and be conducted round by the owner in a four wheel drive vehicle. You can learn about the processing of cocoa beans, and enjoy the lush vegetation of the rain forest from which the plantation was cleared ☎ 453-1260.

The main road then continues through La Caye and Grand Rivère, before winding its way back north into Castries. It is 33 miles (53km) from Vieux Fort to Castries along the east coast route.

As you head back to Castries you will pass **Morne la Combe** on your left. While it is worth stopping a while to take in the views, it is a good idea to set

93

Dennery

more time aside to explore this wonderfiil area. You can take the **Barre de L'isle Rain Forest Trail** which ascends to 1,446 feet at the summit of Mome Ia Combe. The walk takes about three hours and is worth every minute for the lush scenery, wildlife and spectacular views from the top.

NORTH OF CASTRIES

The road north out of Castries goes past Vigie Airport and Vigie Beach, Vide Bouteille Point and Choc Bay with its great beach. Close to the beach is the **Gablewoods Shopping Mall** and along the beach are a number of hotels and resorts, including the luxurious all inclusive Sandals Halcyon. The Mall has a number of eateries and shops including Bodyline, Grasshopper arts and crafts, Colletta's Boutique, Leather 'n Scents, C17 with designer jeans and so on, Augustin Jewellers, and Paramount Associates, the island's authorised dealer for Radio Shack.

Pigeon Point and Rodney Bay

Close to the Sandals Halcyon is the start of the self-guiding **Union Nature Trail**. It is an easy stroll through rain forest flora and fauna. This is an easy looped trail along a graveled path through the rainforest. You can usually see humming-birds and a wealth of other birdlife. You may even be lucky if you are quiet and spot the rare St. Lucia parrot.

The trail starts at the Interpretive Centre at the Union Agricultural Centre that is inland from Choc Bay on the Babonneau road. The medicinal herb garden is fascinating especially as bush medicine is becoming increasingly accepted in alternative medicine. You can also see some of the animals that inhabit the island in the Union Mini Zoo.

GROS ISLET

Gros Islet is most famous for the Friday night 'jump ups', a huge party which spills out into the street and attracts thousands for the carnival-like festivities.

No one is quite sure how the Friday night party started, but some bars decided to put speakers outside in order to attract more customers, this drew people on to the streets and the locals shut the main road to traffic so that it would not interfere with their dancing. Word got around about the Friday night party and soon people were flocking to it from around the island — and they still do.

The party starts around 9pm, and there is deafening music and scores of street stalls selling local specialities such as crispy fried fish, conch, fish cakes, roast corn and little cakes. The bars even set up tables and chairs in the street, and the idea is to mingle, to move from bar to bar enjoying a few beers and a lot of talking and dancing. The party continues until the early hours of Saturday morning, so make sure you have a lift home.

During the rest of the week, the town with its few streets mostly of tiny clapboard houses, goes back to fishing which is its major industry, although tourism is increasingly important as cruise ships are now regular visitors to the town so that passengers can visit the nearby Pigeon Island historic park.

For a brief time during the French Revolution, Gros Islet adopted the name of Revolution. The town does have some attractive larger homes, especially along the beach, and most of the homes have gardens bursting with flowers and fruit trees.

Also inland from Choc Bay and a little to the north, are the **Tropica Gardens** in Monchy. The landscaped gardens are on a private estate and worth visiting for their beautiflil plants and flowers. (☎ 452-0661).

Off the beach is the curiously named **Rat Island**, a former nunnery, that is now being considered for an artists colony.

This stretch of coastline between Vigie and Pigeon Island in the north has many of the island's finest beaches, and is the major resort area.

The road past Gablewoods runs through the huge Marisule Estate and then runs to **Rodney Bay**, one of the most popular haunts for yachts in the Caribbean. The beautifully-landscaped marina has restaurants, bars, shops, yacht chandlery and usually, hundreds of moored vessels. Rodney Bay is now one of the leading charter centres in the Caribbean and several charter companies are based there.

The Rodney Bay Mall has 50 air-conditioned shops plus bank, post office, photolab and large modern supermarket.

Across Rodney Bay is the fishing town of **Gros Islet** with its large Catholic church, and historic Pigeon Point over the bay.

PIGEON ISLAND NATIONAL LANDMARK

Just north of Gros Islet and jutting out into the Caribbean is **Pigeon Point**, formerly **Pigeon Island** and one of the region's most famous historic places (open daily 9am-5pm). It was here in 1782 that Admiral Rodney set sail to intercept the French fleet, and the ensuing **Battle of the Saints** prevented the French from making their rendezvous with the Spanish and saved Jamaica for the British Empire.

Pigeon Point is now connected to the mainland by a causeway built from earth removed during the excavation of the ill-fated Rodney Bay Development, a tourism project that foundered in the 1970s. There is a spectacular drive along the causeway to the parking area at the entrance to the huge fortified area. Even if you are not really interested in history, it is a delightful place to visit.

The causeway is now home to many of St Lucia's luxury hotels, including Sandals Grande.

Pigeon Point covers 44 acres (18 hectares) of sloping grasslands, dry tropical forests, beaches and two peaks connected by a saddle which made excellent observation posts. The area has been beautifully restored by the St Lucia National Trust (with generous assistance from the Canadian Government and others) as a National Landmark, and is in every sense a living museum.

MUSEUM AND PARK

The **museum** and **interpretation centre** in the restored officers quarters has computer-controlled multi-media displays, and is one of the best in the Caribbean. It makes an excellent starting point for your visit. The museum is open daily from 9am-5pm. Admission is EC$5 for adults and EC$0.50 for children.

There are displays about the fort and its development, accounts of the Battle of the Saints, and a history of the area. You can then spend a very pleasant day exploring. Apart from the history of the island, there is a diverse animal and plant life to be enjoyed in the botanic gardens, and if you want a rest, there are beautiful sandy beaches to laze on, a restaurant with good food and incredible views, and even a **200-year-old English tavern**.

The park has proved enormously popular with St Lucians and visitors alike. Many local couples choose to get married there and the park has built a wedding gazebo and has its own wedding coordinator to ensure everything goes smoothly.

The park is well laid out with lots of clear signposting and after entering take the first path to your right, just after the **officer's kitchens**, to visit the museum and interpretive centre.

Then head for the **soldiers' barracks** and the **two gun battery** behind, before returning to the main path and a cluster of buildings which used to be **cooperage**, **bakery** and **commanding officer's quarters**. The path runs westwards past the old **lime kiln**, **jetty** and more soldiers' barracks on your left, to **the U.S. Signal Station**. From here there are a number of paths.

Ahead is the path up to Fort Rodney, to the north is the climb up to **Signal Peak** past gun batteries, and to the south is the trail which heads down to the coastline and leads to the **Carib Caves**. There is a path back along the coast which takes you to the two sheltered sandy beach areas beyond the jetty.

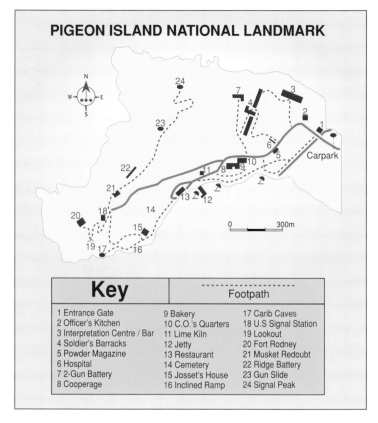

PIGEON ISLAND NATIONAL LANDMARK

Key — Footpath

1 Entrance Gate
2 Officer's Kitchen
3 Interpretation Centre / Bar
4 Soldier's Barracks
5 Powder Magazine
6 Hospital
7 2-Gun Battery
8 Cooperage
9 Bakery
10 C.O.'s Quarters
11 Lime Kiln
12 Jetty
13 Restaurant
14 Cemetery
15 Josset's House
16 Inclined Ramp
17 Carib Caves
18 U.S Signal Station
19 Lookout
20 Fort Rodney
21 Musket Redoubt
22 Ridge Battery
23 Gun Slide
24 Signal Peak

PRE-HISTORY

Pigeon Island used to be part of the mainland and its rock formations are similar to those found elsewhere on St Lucia dating from the Tertiary Period, between 40 and 80 million years old.

It is thought that the island was separated from the mainland about 40,000 years ago during a massive volcanic eruption.

Human activity over centuries removed much of the natural vegetation from the island and this seriously reduced wildlife habitats. A replanting programme is now under way, although indigenous flora can still be seen on steep inaccessible slopes. The island does support, however, a large population of lizards, insects and birds.

The island's first settlers were the pre-historic Amerindians, and artifacts of stone, shell and clay have been found along the eastern shore, dating from around AD 1000. There is some evidence of Arawak influence, but they are likely to have been ousted by the Caribs who preferred to fish, hunt and forage in the lush forests which would then still have covered the island.

FRENCH VS ENGLISH, AGAIN

The first Europeans to visit the island were probably pirates in the 16th century. The infamous Francois Leclerc, who because of his wooden leg was known as **Le Capitaine Jambe de Bois**, is thought to have used it as a hide-out in the 1550s. In 1554 he is known to have captured four galleons. His lieutenant, Jacques Soires, achieved notoriety by capturing Havana and holding the city hostage for three weeks until a huge ransom was paid.

The pirates favoured Pigeon Island because their ships could shelter safely in the bay with look-outs on the peaks giving ample warning of approaching vessels. When the pirate ships sailed out to attack passing vessels, they had the wind behind them which increased their speed and the element of surprise.

On 17 December 1722, a party from an English vessel landed on the island. The ship, commanded by Nathaniel Uring, had been sent by the Duke of Montagu to establish colonies on St Lucia and St Vincent. According to Uring's log, they anchored in Pigeon Island Bay and sent a landing party ashore after spotting several men on the island. It turned out they had canoed across from Martinique to hunt.

"Strategic importance"

The first reference to the island is on a French map of 1717, which named it Gros Islet — the Big Island. The strategic importance of the island was quickly realised. It dominated and protected the bay which later took its name, the northern side of the island was protected by steep cliffs up to 200ft (61m) high, and on the western side, there were only two landing places among the steep rocks. The northern shore is very exposed with constant surf which has swells up to 20ft (6m), while the south-east shore, with its sandy beaches, is usually calm.

He then surveyed the island from sea, and concluded that the "barren, sandy soil" and wind-tossed anchorage made the island unsuitable. The next day they sailed further south to look for a better site.

In 1778 the French declared war on the English in support of the American War of Independence, and an English fleet immediately attacked and captured St Lucia. A naval base was established in Gros Islet Bay, protected by the heavily fortified Pigeon Island. In 1779 two English fleets under the command of Rear Admiral the Hon. Samuel Barrington and Vice Admiral Sir John Byron gathered off Pigeon Island in one of the largest Royal Navy forces ever gathered in the Caribbean. The fleet consisting of 23 battleships and 10 frigates, started to harass the French fleet operating out of Martinique. Among the English naval commanders were Admirals Hyde-Parker, Rodney, Hood and Drake.

On 16 December, Parker's squadron sailed out, intercepted and destroyed most of a French convoy sailing through the St Lucia Channel trying to reach Fort Royal. Three French frigates were captured and Hyde-Parker was app-ointed senior naval officer at Pigeon Island.

There were several engagements between English and French warships during the early part of 1779, but the French were unable to dislodge the English from Pigeon Island and in April, Admiral Rodney arrived with reinforcements and took command.

In April 1780 the *HMS Cornwall* was scuttled at Carenage, and the *HMS Fame* sank in Gros Islet Bay after an engagement in which both sides suffered heavy losses. When the Spanish fleet under Admiral Don José Selena joined forces with the French in Fort Royal, Rodney set about fortifying Pigeon Island even more. The extra defences discouraged the Spanish and French fleets who sailed out of the area. Rodney sailed with most of his warships to the coast of North America.

A small squadron was left to defend Pigeon Island, and during 11 and 12 October 1780 the worst recorded hurricane to hit the West Indies struck St Lucia, crippling the English fleet, sinking many vessels and doing massive damage on Pigeon Island. Rodney headed back with his fleet, arriving in December.

Skirmishes between the English and French fleets continued in 1781 and in May, a French invasion force was driven out of Gros Islet Bay after a ferocious bombardment from Pigeon Island. The naval activity in the region finally concluded with the **Battle of the Saints**, by far the most significant naval action in the Caribbean, and of enormous political importance to the then world order.

The battle got its name because it was fought off the Isles des Saintes between Guadeloupe and Dominica. The French fleet in Fort Royal, Martinique, planned to connect with the Spanish fleet at Cap Francois in Haiti, and then launch an attack on Fort Charles in Jamaica, then commanded by Admiral Horatio Nelson. If successful, the combined French and Spanish attack could have driven the English out of the Caribbean.

Admiral Rodney's reinforced fleet in 1782, numbered 36 ships of the line, and more than 70 armed support vessels. Lookouts on Pigeon Island were able to monitor the French build up at Fort Royal, and on 8 April, Rodney received a signal that the French fleet of more than 150 ships and an army of 10,000 men, had set sail. Within two hours, the English fleet was also under way and in pursuit.

The French were anxious to avoid a confrontation until they could link up with the Spanish fleet, but Rodney knew he would be outnumbered if this happened.

For three days, the French fleet eluded the English, but their ships slowed down on the evening of 11 April because of

L'armee Francais dan les bois

After the French Revolution, the slaves on St Lucia were given their freedom. Realising that the island would probably revert to the English and slavery be re-introduced, they banded together as '**l'armee Francais dan les bois**'. They carried widespread destruction on the island in what is known as the Brigands War, and in 1795, although heavily fortified, they captured Pigeon Island for a short time. A peace treaty was agreed between the English and the Brigands in 1798. Pigeon Island was restored and served as Naval Headquarters until the Treaty of Paris in 1814.

THE ARTIST OF ST LUCIA – LLEWELLYN XAVIER

Llewellyn Xavier is St Lucia's most famous and innovative artist. Born in Choiseul in 1945, he became an agricultural apprentice and went to Barbados in 1961, where a friend gave him a box of watercolour paints. He started to paint and his genius was immediately apparent.

His first exhibition was a sell out and he rapidly established an international reputation. In 1968 he moved to England and created Mail Art, a new concept in modern art which attracted critical acclaim. His work has been exhibited in most of the world's leading galleries, but in 1979, at the age of 34, he enrolled as a student at the School of the Museum of Fine Art in Boston as a student. It was a time of great spiritual awakening, and for a time he became a Benedictine monk in Montreal having sold all his worldly possessions. He realised, however, that art was his life and in 1987 he married and returned to St Lucia.

He was a founder member of the St Lucia Environmental Development and Awareness Council, which opposed unwelcome tourism development.

This concern with the environment led to his masterpiece entitled Global Council for the Restoration of the Earth's Environment. The work incorporates recycled materials, 18th and 19th century prints of birds, animals, fishes and plants, many of them now extinct, and postage stamps from around the world, as well as the signatures of world environmental leaders and conservationists. The work is on display at his studio, but viewing is by appointment only ☎ 450-9155.

Opposite: Pigeon Island National Landmark has two small beaches and the restaurant shown here

the calmer winds in the lee of Dominica, and overnight Admiral Hood's squadron attacked, disabling two of the French ships as the fleets commanded by Rodney and Drake closed in. The first English barrage wreaked havoc, and although the battle raged all day, Admiral de Grasse on his flagship Ville de Paris, struck his colours in surrender just before sunset.

19TH CENTURY

Many of the buildings were badly damaged by a hurricane in 1817, but some were rebuilt and used as soldiers barracks. Yellow fever struck the garrison in 1842 killing many of the soldiers. It was finally abandoned in 1861 and all the guns sold and removed from the island. In 1878 the island was used as a holding camp for East Indian indentured labourers until they could be placed on the estates. In 1901 when a yellow fever epidemic again hit St Lucia, troops stationed at the Morne Battery outside Castries moved to Pigeon Island and stayed until 1904, when it was abandoned as a military base for the last time.

20TH CENTURY

In 1909 a whaling station was opened on the island, and in the 1920s a small fleet of American-owned whaling schooners was based there. In 1925, however, St Lucia enacted legislation to control whaling around the island.

Yet another colourful episode in the island's history occurred on 31 March 1937 when **Josset Agnes Hutch-inson**, an actress with the D'Oyle Carte Operetta Company, secured a lease for Pigeon Island. Although she had to leave the island during the American occupation during the Second World War, she returned in 1947 and established a yacht station, which earned a worldwide reputation because of her charm and lavish hospitality. With the launch of the Rodney Bay development, which included Pigeon Island, in 1970 she had to surrender her lease, but was able to retain an acre of land around her home, where she lived until 1976 when she returned to England. She died in 1978 at the age of 90.

US PRESENCE

Pigeon Island was chosen by the Americans in 1940 as one of several bases in the region aimed at protecting the Panama Canal. President Franklin Roosevelt arrived aboard the *USS Tuscaloosa* on 8 December, personally to inspect the base which included Pigeon Island and surrounding land. On 1 Feb-ruary 1941, the base was commissioned as a **Naval Air Station** with a squadron of 18 flying boats, and it was also an important communications station with the code name Peter Item. The base on Pigeon Island was decommissioned on 1 June 1947 and the land returned to the St Lucia Government.

THE CAUSEWAY

The causeway to the island was completed in 1973 as part of the Rodney Bay development project, and the St Lucia National Trust undertook as one of its first priorities to create a national park on Pigeon Point as it was now known. The park was officially opened by Princess Alexandria on 23 February 1979, to commemorate the island's independence attained the previous day. It was the venue for the climax of the Independence Celebrations.

REFRESHMENTS

The **Beach Cafe Jambe de Bois** is named after the famous pirate Francois Leclerc. The restaurant is beside the sea and looks out over Rodney Bay. You can enjoy a quick snack or more leisurely meal with Creole and barbecue cooking.

The **Captain's Cellar** is beneath the faithfully reconstructed officers Mess and has been furnished to resemble an English tavern at the beginning of the 19th century. It offers light snacks, drinks and some amazing cocktails!

The Shop overlooks the Atlantic Ocean and sells souvenirs, St Lucia handicrafts and Pigeon Island mementoes.

NORTH OF PIGEON POINT

From Pigeon point you can drive north to **Pointe Du Cap**. This northern tip of the island contains the 1,500 acre (600 hectare) Cap Estate, many fine beaches and coves, golf course, and some of St Lucia's most expensive homes which have fabulous views over the seas. Martinique can be seen clearly on the horizon. While in the Cap Estate, visit the gallery of local artist **Llewelyn Xavier**. His works and those of other St Lucian and Caribbean artists are on display.

There is a wonderful walk from hardy Point through the

Above: Part of the former British Navy defences at Pigeon Island

Below: The picturesque north-west coast

aptly named cactus Valley to Pigeon island. You can either return to Castries along the coast road, enjoying a leisurely lunch at one of the beach grills and a swim in the sea, or take the inland road south of Gros Islet which runs past Mount Monier to **Barbonneau** and then west back into Castries. You can experience the traditional St Lucian way of life by visiting the **Fond Latisab Creol Park**. The Park is one of 14 members of Heritage Tours Explore St Lucia which aims to provide islanders and visitors alike with a unique view of the island's heritage.

At Fond Latisab you can see and taste how traditional cassava bread is made. You can watch acrobatic foresters saw through huge logs using centuries-old cross cut saws and see how the locals use woven lobster pots to catch delicious fresh water crayfish.

Whats encouraging is that the heritage center is especially popular with local school children who can hear about the island's traditions and culture and also experience traditional creole songs and dance. One of their favorite songs refers to the habit of using coconut fiber as mattress stuffing. It goes "Oh help me, I cannot sleep the coconut fiber is pricking me."

The center is open daily from Monday to Friday and Sundays 8am-4pm. (☎ 450-6327).

Just south of Mount Monier, the road runs close to what used to be the Morne Paix Bouche Estate, where it is claimed, the young Empress Josephine was born in 1763. Her family lived at Paix Bouche until 1771 when they moved to Martinique, although she spent much of her childhood in the south of the island around Soufrière.

There are a number of other bays on the north-eastern coastline which are accessible, such as the sweeping Grande Anse and Anse Lavoutte, these all offer interesting days out, especially with a picnic lunch.

EATING OUT –
NORTH OF CASTRIES

Barefoot by the Sea
Inside Sandals Grande St. Lucian
(☎ 455-2000)
New to addSpeciality restaurant
and grill located directly on the
beach offering Latin and
Caribbean fare. Reservations not
required.

Bayside $$-$$$ ***
Sandals Halcyon
Choc Bay
(☎ 453-0222)
Outdoor restaurant and bar bt
the pool and beach serving
buffet lunch with an a la carte
menu featuring everything from
sumptuous steaks to sandwiches
and burgers.

Cafe Tropical $-$$ **
Pointe Seraphine
(☎ 452-7411)
A fast food offering snacks, hot
meals and fast foods, as well as
ice cream and draught beer.

Captain's Cellar $-$$
(☎ 452-0918)
18th Century British tavern on
Pigeon Island. Authentic 18th C
fare. Open daily.

Chung's $-$$ **
Sans Soucis
(☎ 452-1499)
A good Chinese restaurant
offering relaxed, casual dining.

D's Restaurant $$ **
Edgewater Beach Hotel,
Vigie Beach
(☎ 453-7931)
A mix of Creole and
international dishes served at
lunch and dinner with good
daily Creole specials. Great for
fish and chicken dishes and a
wonderful place to watch the
sunset. There are daily lunch
specials, and dine out on the
terrace with excellent seafood,
and specialities such as sauteed
chicken livers in sherry, and
chicken picatta with mint and
yoghurt.

Dragonfly
Windjammer Landing
(☎ 456-9000)
The best of the 'East' merges
with the finest of the 'West' in a
fusion of Caribbean and Asian
cuisine. Try cilantro-cured tuna
with wasabi sauce tuna or sugar
cane Mahi Mahi. Dinner
reservations required for fine
waterfront dining.

Inexpensive $ Moderate $$ *Expensive $$$*
The * system (from one to four) is based on quality of food, service and ambience.

Friendship Inn $-$$ **
Sunny Acres
(☎ 452-4201)
Charming and friendly little
restaurant for breakfast and
dinner. Good value for money,
There are barbecues by the pool
on Saturday nights.

Jammers Beach Bar $-$$ **
Windjammer Landing
(☎ 452-9000)
All day casual beachside dining.

Laurell's Restaurant $-$$ **
Bois d'Orange (☎ 452-8547)
Creole specialities in an informal
setting. Daily specials.

Mario's $$-$$$ ***
Sandals Halcyon,
Choc Bay
(☎ 453-0222)
A gourmet restaurant offering
the finest of Italian fare, with
excellent fresh pasta dishes and
a good Italian wine list. Open
for dinner only. Reservations are
not required.

Olde London Pub and Restaurant
Inside Sandals Grande St. Lucian
(☎ 455-2000)
Savour your choice of English
cooking in a genuine old English
setting complete with pool table
and darts.

Papa Don's $$ **
Windjammer Landing
(☎ 452-9000)
Mediterranean style taverna
offering great pizza from wood
burning ovens, fresh pasta and a
selection of Italian dishes.
Spectacular views of Martinique
can be seen from the
mountainside terrace.

The Pierhouse Restaurant $$-$$$ ***
Sandals Halcyon,
Choc Bay
(☎ 453-0222)
Dine in elegance and splendour
in the restaurant which is built
over the sea. The restaurant
offers the best of island cooking.
Reservations required.
Serving dinner only.
Open from 6.30pm to 11pm.

La Pomme Cannelle $$-$$$ ***
Glencastle Resort
(☎ 450-0833)
Caribbean and continental
cuisine.

(cont'd)

109

EATING OUT –
NORTH OF CASTRIES (cont'd)

Toscanini's
In Sandals Grande St. Lucian
Pigeon island causeway
(☎ 455-2000)
New to addA classic Italian
restaurant located on the lower
level and facing the sea.
Reservations not required.

Upper Deck
Windjammer Landing
(☎ 456-9000)
New to addChic seafood bistro
with an ocean view. In addition
to sumptuous seafood try grilled
steaks, kebabs, salads and
sandwiches. Daily 'Captains
Table' menu also available.

The Wharf Restaurant & Bar
$-$$ *
Choc Beach
(☎ 450-4844)
Light fare and snacks.
Open 10am-1am.

GABLEWOODS
SHOPPING MALL

(nearly opposite Sandals Halcyon)

The Sub-Station
(☎ 451-7300)
Creole food.

RODNEY BAY –
GROS INLET

The Big Chef Steak House
$-$$ *
Next to the Mall in Rodney Bay.
(☎ 450-0210)
Specialises in char-grilled,
hickory flavoured, Angus steaks.
Also serves seafood, salad and
pasta. Open Monday to
Saturday.

Bosun's Bar & Bistro $$ *
Rodney Bay Marina
(☎ 458-4190)
Perfect for pizza, burgers and
ribs or pasta and salads.

Boatyard Pub
The gap before Bank of St. Lucia
Rodney Bay Marina.
(☎ 715-5458)
New to addBar and bistro
serving lunch and dinner
Monday to Sunday.

Buzz Seafood & Grill
$$-$$$ *
Rodney Bay
(☎ 458-0450)
Seafood, steaks, and vegetarian
specialities. Enjoy potato
crusted Red Snapper, baked

EATING OUT –
RODNEY BAY - GROS ISLET

Dorado filled with avocado, Moroccan spiced lamb shanks or BBQ baby back ribs. Dine inside or in the "Secret Garden". Happy hour 5 – 7pm. Open every day from December 1 to March 31. Closed on Mondays from March 31 to November 30th.

Cafe Claude $$ **
Rodney Bay
(☎ 458-0847)
An oasis of calm in the middle of busy Rodney Bay village. Open every day from breakfast until late. The bar offers cocktails, fine wines, freshly squeezed local juices and imported beers. Dinner offers an eclectic fusion of European and Caribbean cuisine.

Cafe Olé & Elena's Ice Cream $-$$ **
Rodney Bay
(☎ 458-0576/452-8726)
freshly made sandwhiches and snacks and delicious homemade Italian ice cream and sorbets.

Cats Whiskers $$ **
Rodney Bay
(☎ 452-8880)
Home cooked English food in a friendly atmosphere. Open 6 days a week. Located at the ramp on Reduit Beach.

Capone's $-$$ **
Rodney Bay
(☎ 452-0284)
Elegant air conditioned dining experience in a 1920's setting. Taste of the Caribbean blends Mediterranean cuisine with fresh, local ingredients. La Piazza on the terrace serves pasta, pizza, seafood, steaks and salads. Open 5pm – 12 midnight. Closed on Mondays.

Charthouse $$-$$$ ****
Rodney Bay
(☎ 452-8115)
Good food in a beautiful luxurious greenhouse setting beside the water. Noted for its charcoal broiled-steaks, hickory smoked spare ribs and fresh, locally caught seafood. Specialities include lobster in season, stuffed crab backs and callaloo soup. Open seven days a week. Reservations are recommended. Take out service also available.

(cont'd)

EATING OUT –
RODNEY BAY - GROS ISLET

Chic
Royal St. Lucian
(☎ 452-9999)
Combines delicious food,
beautiful surroundings and great
service. Cool and sophisticated
accenting art, music and
wonderful food.

The Dog House
Rodney Bay
(☎ 452-0054)
Enjoy Tex Mex food and country
and western music. Happy hour
6-7.30pm. Open every day.

Eagles Inn $-$$ ***
Rodney Bay
(☎ 452-0650)
Famous for its freshly caught
seafood dishes and West Indian
lamb dishes. The waterfront inn
is open for lunch and dinner and
snacks in between, and offers
island specialities such as
callaloo, curry and accras (fish
cakes). There is nightly evening
entertainment including a Creole
dance night and traditional
barbecue. Sunday is "eat all you
can" family day. Open Sunday
to Thursday from 10am, Friday
10am-5pm, and Saturday from
5pm.

The Golden Apple $$ ***
Gros Islet
(☎ 450-8056)
Only Creole and seafood
specialities, including lobster,
barbecued lambi and chicken,
are offered in this small,
intimate restaurant which opens
for dinner. Try the conch, flying
fish and rotis.

**The Great House
$$-$$$** ****
Cap Estate
(☎ 450-0450)
Renowned for its elegant
ambience and excellent cuisine
this restored great house once
hosted Admiral Horatio Nelson.
Retaining old colonial charm and
offering an extensive a la carte
menu, changing every two
months, guests can experience
fine dining in a glorious setting.
Afternoon tea is served from
4.30 – 5.30pm, happy hour
starts at 5.50pm and dinner is
from 6.30–9.45pm. Reservations
advisable.

(cont'd)

Hooters
Rodney Bay
(☎ 466-8377)
Lively late night bar and restaurant.
Inexpensive snacks include fajitas, buffalo wings, spare ribs and burgers. Advertised as serving the tastefully tacky.

Key Largo $-$$ **
Rodney Bay Marina
(☎ 452-0282)
Proper pizzas cooked the traditional way in wood-fired ovens, plus good salads, great coffee and an interesting Italian wine list. Happy Hour is between 5.30-6.30pm.

L'Epicure Restaurant and Mistral Lounge $$-$$$ ***
Royal St Lucian,
Rodney Bay
(☎ 452-9999)
The beachside restaurant specialises in fresh seafood and West Indian dishes, the Monday night Caribbean buffet features local specialities accompanied by a steel drum band. After dinner you can enjoy cocktails while listening to the Royal's resident jazz band. Open daily from 7pm-10pm. Le Mistral Lounge is open until midnight.

The Lime Restaurant, Bar and Nightclub $$ ***
Opposite the Papillon Hotel
Rodney Bay
(☎ 452-0761)
Good value food, great setting and one of the fun places on the island. You can enjoy an open air breakfast, an excellent value for money Creole buffet lunch or bar snacks, and a delicious dinner before working it off on the dance floor. The seafood is always good. Dinner is served from 6.30-11pm, and the restaurant specialises in locally caught seafood and charcoal grilled steaks. The Late Lime, the night club, offers a wide choice of music from classical reggae and calypso to country and jazz, as well as Karaoke. Friday and Saturday are disco nights and Sunday jazz night. Closed on Tuesdays.
Happy hour 5.30 – 6.30pm.

(cont'd)

EATING OUT –
RODNEY BAY - GROS ISLET

Memories of Hong Kong
**$-$$ **

Reduit-Gros Islet Highway
Opposite Royal St. Lucian Hotel
Rodney Bay
(☎ 452-8218)
Authentic Cantonese and
Chinese cooking prepared by
their resident chef from Hong
Kong. There are lots of speciality
dishes, including a vegetarian
bird's nest soup, and delicious
freshly made desserts. There is
an open kitchen so you can see
your food being prepared. Open
from 4.30pm Monday to
Saturday.

The Oriental $$-$$$
Rex St Lucian
(☎ 452-8351)
Fine dining and exotic oriental
cuisine.

Pizza! Pizza! $ *
Rodney Bay
(☎ 452-8282)
Best pizza on the island.
Waterside garden dining and
children's playground.

Razmataz Tandoori Restaurant
**$$ **

Opposite Royal St. Lucian Hotel,
Rodney Bay.
(☎ 452-9800)
The island's first Indian Tandoori
restaurant. Open from 4pm.
Close on Tuesdays.

Snooty Agouti $-$$ **
Rodney Bay
Pigeon Island, Gros Islet.
(☎ 452-0321)
Eat and enjoy the art in this
restaurant/gallery/shop.

Spinnakers Beach Bar
and Grill $-$$ **
St Lucia Yacht Club,
Reduit Beach
(☎ 452-8491)
Situated on the water's edge of
beautiful Reduit Beach. The
restaurant serves breakfast,
lunch and dinner with great
views of the bay. Apart from the
excellent carvery, the
blackboard menu offers a good
choice at very reasonable prices.

(cont'd)

Tao
Body Holiday at LeSport
Cariblue Beach
(☎ 450-8551)
A nutritious and delicious dining experience. Contemporary dishes with an unexpected combination of flavours in an elegant setting.

Scuttlebutts Bar & Grill
Rodney Bay Marina
(☎ 452-0351)
Tavern style waterside dining. Open daily for bar snacks, beer by the bucket, wines and cocktails. Scuttlebutts has a swimming pool and a communications centre with fast internet connection.

Tilly's 2x4 Restaurant & Bar
$$ *
Rodney Heights
(☎ 458-4440)
St. Lucia's only authentic Creole Restaurant and Cabawe.

The Villa
Rodney Bay
(☎ 452-9199)
Located at the Caribbean Jewel Beach resort the Villa is open for breakfast, lunch and dinner. Has one of the finest views in Rodney Bay.

Fact File

ARRIVAL, ENTRY REQUIREMENTS AND CUSTOMS

An immigration form has to be filled in and presented on arrival. The form requires you to say where you will be staying on the island, and if you plan to move around, put down the first hotel you will be staying at. The immigration form is in two parts, one of which is stamped and returned to you in your passport. You must retain this until departure when the slip is retrieved as you check in at the airport.

British citizens and those from European Community and Commonwealth countries need a valid passport for entry, but a visa is not required. You may also be asked to show that you have a return ticket before being admitted. Visitors from the United States and Canada staying less than six months can enter on an I.D. card but must have valid return tickets.

If travelling on business, a letter confirming this, may prove helpful in speeding your way through customs, especially if travelling with samples.

Having cleared immigration, you will have to go through customs, and it is quite usual to have to open your luggage for inspection. If you have expensive cameras, jewellery, etc it is a good idea to travel with a photocopy of the receipt. The duty free allowance entering St Lucia is 200 cigarettes or 250 grams of tobacco or 50 cigars, and one litre of spirit or wine. There is duty free shopping at Pointe Seraphine and in the departure lounge of Hewanorra Airport.

ACCOMMODATION

The free and widely available 'Road Map St Lucia' locates all hotels and resorts on the island.

St Lucia has a wide range of accommodation to suit all tastes and pockets, from the five star all-inclusive resorts to inns, modest guesthouses, self-catering apartments and beach cottages.

All inclusive resorts such as Club St Lucia, Jalousie Plantation Resort, Sandals and Windjammer Landing, are just that, the price covers everything including drinks and all facilities. The service is first class and prices reflect this.

If you want to eat out and explore quite a lot, it may pay to stay in a hotel offering part board, or one of the many inns on the island, some of them converted plantation homes, and generally offering excellent value for money.

There are also apartments, holiday villas and beach cottages available for rent offering you the privacy of your own accommodation and the flexibility to eat in or out.

Some terms: MAP stands for Modified American Plan i.e. breakfast and dinner are included. EP or European Plan means bed only and no meals. CP is Continental Plan which is bed and breakfast, and AP for American Plan, means room and all meals. Prices quoted by hotels are for rooms, whether one or two people are sharing, and you may find it difficult to get a reduction if you are travelling alone, but have a go. Prices, unless clearly stated, do not usually include the 8 per cent Government tax and 10 per cent service charge. $ represents inexpensive accommodation, $$ moderate, and $$$ de-luxe.

AN A-Z OF ACCOMMODATION

Anse Chastanet Beach Hotel $$
PO Box 7000, Soufrière
☎/Fax: 459-7000
Near the famous Pitons on the sheltered western shore of the island, with spacious hillside and beachside accommodation. Facilities include two restaurants and bars, two beaches, scuba, spa, boutiques, jungle biking, free hiking pro-gramme for walkers and nature lovers, water sports, airport transportation, tennis and organised trips. Children under the age of 4 are not accommodated.

Auberge Seraphine $-$$
Castries
☎ 453-2073
Good value 28-room hotel over looks Vigie Yacht Marina.

Balenbouche Estate $$
Balenbouche Bay
☎ 455-1244
Comfortable rooms 8 in the Great House and two adjoining cottages set in a 150-acre plantation.

Bay Gardens Hotel $$
Rodney Bay
☎ 452-8060
Good location with 71 rooms and 8 mini-suites, plus restaurant and conference center. An award wining intimate hotel.

Calabash Cove Inn and Sanctuary
Marisule
☎ 450-3302
Calabash Cove enjoys an idyllic setting in the bay of Bonaire estate in the north west corner of the island. This new venture consists of 23 one-bedroom villas with large living rooms. The villas have roman baths, outdoor rain showers, lanai's with hammocks, cable TV and phones with I-net.

Cara Suites $$
Close to Castries
☎ 452-4767
Nestled in the hills above Castries and just 5 minutes from the airport. Warm hospitality, superior service and value for money. 54 air-conditioned rooms. Complimentary shuttles to Castries and the beach.

Caribbean Jewel Beach Resort
Rodney Bay
☎ 452-9199
Ideal location with great views of Rodney Bay, Pigeon Island and neighbouring Martinique. Close to Reduit Beach and all the amenities of Rodney Bay Village and the marina. 30 rooms all with views of bay and Caribbean sea.

Club St Lucia by Splash $$$ – all inclusive
PO Box 915, Castries
☎ 450-0551
(UK 0372-66944, US 212-545-8437, Canada 416-968-9500)
On the northern tip of the private Cap Estate, the resort has more than 372 bungalows spaced through the scenic hillside gardens. Facilities include racquet club with courts, gym, squash court and pool. The resort offers 2 restaurants and bars, beach bar, 3 pools, two beaches, tennis, boutiques, drug store and children's club. Rates include accommodation, drinks, meals, water and

land sports, tennis, nightly entertainment, government and service taxes.

Coco Kreole $
Rodney Bay
☎ 452-0744
St Lucia's newest small hotel. 20 intimate rooms recently renovated.

Daphil Mini Hotel $$
Gros Islet
☎ 450-9318
A 10 room hotel.

East Winds Inn $$-$$$
– all inclusive
Labrellotte Bay,
PO Box 193, Castries
☎ 452-8212
A small 30 chalet resort set in tropical gardens, between Castries and Cap Estate with a reef sheltered beach ideal for snorkelling. Facilities include restaurant, clubhouse, bars, pool with sunk-in bar, sun terrace and snorkelling equipment.

Fox Grove Inn $
Mon Repos Post Office,
St Lucia
☎ 455-3800
A comfortable 12 room inn with magnificent views of Praslin Bay on the eastern Atlantic coast, about 20 minutes drive from Hewanorra Airport. Facilities include fine restaurant, bars, pool, tennis. clubhouse, horse riding, nature walks, shuttle bus to the beach about 1 mile (2km) away.

Friendship Inn $
Sunny Acres,
PO Box 1475, Castries
☎ 452-4201
A small 10 room hotel 3 miles (5km) from Castries and within easy walking distance of the beach, shops and restaurants. Facilities include restaurant, bar and pool.

Ginger Lily $$
Rodney Bay
☎ 458-0300
A small intimate 11 room hotel close to the beach with pool and internet cafe. Self catering is possible.

Glencastle Resort $
PO Box 143, Massade,
Gros Islet, Castries
☎ 450-0833
A 37 room hotel overlooking Rodney Bay marina, close to two beaches and with conference facilities for the business visitor. Facilities include pool and gazebo bar and restaurant. Nearby facilities include golf and riding stables.

Golden Arrow Inn $
PO Box 2037, Marisule,
Gros Islet, Castries
☎ 450-1832
A friendly, small family owned and managed 15 room inn aimed at the budget traveller, with beaches nearby. Faclities include bar, water sports and golf.

Green Parrot Inn $-$$
Casties,
☎ 452-3399
A friendly and lively inn with 53 rooms, and famous for its restaurant and views from its vantage point on the Morne. Facilities include popular nightclub and pool.

Harbour Light Inn $
City Gate, C/o LaClery
Post Office, Castries,
☎ 452-9455
On Vigie Beach and close to downtown Castries. Facilities include restaurant and bar, with beaches and shopping nearby.

Harmony Suites $$-$$$
Rodney Bay
☎ 452-8756
On the waterfront and close to beaches. 30 luxury suites, restau-

rant, bar, pool, mini mart and water sports.

Humming Bird Beach Resort $$

PO Box 280, Soufrière
☎ 459-7232
A small resort set in tropical gardens running down to the beach. Facilities include restaurant, bar, pool, beach and batik studio.

JJ's Paradise Resort $$

Marigot Bay
☎ 451-4076
A 10 room resort with restaurant and pool.

Juliette's Lodge $

Vieux Fort
☎ 454-5300
A comfortable 22 room inn with restaurant and pool.

Inn on The Bay $$

Marigot Bay
☎ 451-4260
An exclusive, small hotel with just 5 rooms and a very intimate atmosphere.

Jalousie Hilton Spa Resort $$$

PO Box 251, Soufrière
☎ 456-8000
(UK 0800-22-761, US and Canada 800-392-2007)
Set in the mountains amid tropical gardens with luxury amenities. Sports activities and instruction, spa and fitness centre, supervised children's activities, airport transfers, and all taxes and service charges. Facilities include 114 rooms, restaurants, bars, watersports, dive shop, tennis, deep sea fishing and sightseeing tours.

Kimatrai Hotel $

PO Box 238, Vieux Fort
☎ 454-6328
A small friendly hotel with a dozen

double rooms, 6 apartments and 3 bungalows a 3 minute drive from Hewanorra Airport. Facilities include restaurant, bar, laundry service and television lounge.

La Haut Plantation Resort $$$

☎ 459-7008
Just north of Soufrière, set in 52 acres of gardens and overlooking the Pitons.

Ladera Resort $$-$$$

Soufrière
☎ 459-7323
Voted the 'Best Small Resort, on the island, it offers 6 villas and 19 suites set in beautiful tropical gardens with stunning views of the Pitons and the Caribbean. Six of the deluxe villas have their own private pools and waterfalls, while 8 suites have their own plunge pools. The restaurant has won a number of awards, and the resort also has a bar, pool, library and nearby watersports.

Le Sport The Body Hotel $$-$$$

PO Box 437,
Cariblue Beach, Castries
☎ 450-8551
(US and Canada 800-544-2883, UK 0800-590-794)
An all inclusive beach resort at the north-west tip of the island, with an emphasis on health, activity and relaxation. Facilities include 155 rooms, 2 restaurants, bar, three pools, beach, Oasis Spa & Ayurvedic Centre, floodlit tennis, cycling, volleyball, archery, hiking, fencing, weight training, golf, aerobics, yoga, stress management and Thai Chi.

Mago Estate Hotel $$$

☎ 459-5880
Just outside Soufrière. Set in tropical gardens and overlooking the Pitons. There are 6 luxury rooms, restaurant and pool.

Fact File

Marigot Beach Club $$
Marigot Bay,
PO Box 101, Castries
☎ 451-4974
9 miles (14km) from Castries with cottages set in the hills behind the marina. Facilities include dive shop, day sailing, pool, water taxi, water sports, yacht charters, restaurants, bars, boutiques and provision store.

Marlin Quay Resort $$-$$$
Rodney Bay Marina
☎ 452-0393
A popular waterfront resort with 40 luxury 1 to 3 bedroom suites, apartment and villas.

Oasis Marigot $$
PO Box 387, Castries
☎ 451-4185
(US and Canada 800-263-4202)
A small, intimate resort of 20 sea houses on the hillsides close to Marigot Bay with stunning views. Each house has direct access to the small palm-fringed beach. Facilities include restaurants, bars, dive shop, day sailing to Soufrière, Rodney Bay and Martinique, water taxi service to deserted beaches, water sports and boutiques.

Palm Tree Hotel $$-$$$
Rodney Bay
☎ 452-8200
A charming setting for this 20-room property which offers privacy and total relaxation. Facilities include the Le Bon Gout restaurant and poolside Carnival Bar, jacuzzi, beauty and hairdressing salon.

Papillon Hotel $$$
Reduit Beach
☎ 452-0984
A luxury all-inclusive 140 room resort formerly part of the Rex St. Lucian property. It offers restaurants, bars, pool, fitness centre, tennis and watersports.

Rainbow Hotel $-$$
Reduit Beach, Rodney Bay
☎ 452-0148
A very comfortable hotel at the northern end of the beach with 76 rooms. It has a restaurant, bar, snack bar, shop and boutique plus Olympic-size pool and children's wading pool.

Rendezvous Resort $$$ – all inclusive
Malabar Beach,
PO Box 190, Castries
☎ 452-4211,
(US 1-800-544-2883)
A chic, couples only resort with luxury cottages set in 7 acres (3 hectares) of tropical gardens alongside a sandy beach. Rates include meals with table wine, drinks, daily activities, sports equipment, airport transfers and all taxes and service charges. Facilities include restaurant, terrace restaurant, bar, tennis, gym, jacuzzi, sauna, water sports, pools, cycling, swim up bar and beach bar.

Rex St Lucian $$-$$$
Reduit Beach,
PO Box 512, Castries
☎ 452-8351
(US 800-223-9868
UK 0208-741-5333)
An all inclusive resort set in 10 acres (4 hectares) of tropical grounds alongside one of the island's finest beaches. The 120 room hotel is a 15 minute drive from Castries. Facilities include mini shopping arcade, tours, activities desk, car rental, restaurants, bars, disco, snorkelling, scuba, pool, tennis and beach.

Royal St Lucian Hotel $$$
Reduit Beach,
PO Box 977, Castries
☎ 452-9999
(US 800-255-5859,
UK 0208-741-5333)

The magnificent Royal St Lucian is situated on the fabulous Reduit Beach and provides the sophistication and elegance of a luxury resort only minutes from the capital of Castries. The classical entrance hall with its cool marble interior, tropical plants and cascading fountain offers a delightful welcome to the weary visitor. Leading through the entrance hall, guests can glimpse the lush vegetation of the gardens with their fabulous pool and swim-up bar.

All the suites offer separate bedrooms and living accommodation with luxury bathrooms and elegant terraces overlooking the gardens and sparkling waters of the Caribbean sea.

The stylish bar is cool and relaxing for pre-dinner drinks which are served to the sounds of a relaxing classical pianist or to soft jazz rhythms. The grace and charm of the staff in L'Epicure is surpassed only by the beautiful surroundings and the delicious menu.

Guests can enjoy the facilities at the adjacent Rex St Lucian with its floodlit tennis courts, shopping plaza and a variety of exciting evening entertainments.

Sandals Grande St Lucian Spa and Beach Resort $$$
Rodney Bay
☎ 455-2000
Sprawling on 17 acres of beautiful beaches between Rodney Bay and Pigeon Island, this luxury, all-inclusive resort offers 280 rooms and suites including 24 Honeymoon Lagoon swim-up rooms. There are 5 gourmet restaurants (14 if you want to try the restaurant at Sandal's other two St. Lucian properties) with live nightly entertainment, nightclub and the island's largest ballroom. Facilities include 4 pools, scuba certification pool, tennis and an array of land and water sports. Golf is available nearby at Sandals St. Lucia Golf Resort and Spa including compli-mentary transfers and green fees. There is a fully-equipped 24-hour fitness center and a full-service European spa with everything from complimentary sauna and steam bath to unique outdoor massage gazebos.

Sandals Halcyon Beach $$$ – all inclusive
Choc Bay
☎ 453-0222, (US 1-800-SANDALS, UK 0207-581-9895)
An all-inclusive couples only luxury resort with cottages set in beautiful landscaped gardens alongside a long, sandy beach. Facilities include 3 restaurants, seven bars and swim up bars, pools, entertainment, daily activities, airport transfers, gift shops, body shop, car rental, disco, fitness centre and health club complex, golf, scuba, tennis, tours and water sports.

Sandals Regency Golf Resort and Spa at La Toc $$$ – all inclusive
La Toc, PO Box 399, Castries
☎ 452-3081
(US 1-800-SANDALS, UK 0207-581-9895)
Another all-inclusive luxury resort (327 rooms) 2 suites with pastel-coloured villas set in tropical gardens on a hillside which descends to a crescent shaped, half mile long beach. Facilities include water sports, pools, including the largest fresh water pool in the Caribbean, 6 restaurants and 10 bars, beachgrill and bar, laundry service, tennis, golf, water sports, fitness centre, gift shop, beauty salon, nightclub and beach vendors market. A $15 million expansion includes the Villa Suites on Sunset Bluff – 56 luxury 1 and 2 storey suites atop a coral buff with breathtaking ocean views. All suites have jacuzzi and 24-hour butler service.

SeaHorse Inn $-$$
Marigot Bay,
PO Box 1825, Castries
☎ 451-4436
Close to a secluded beach with 5
rooms and waterside cottages.
There are several restaurants
nearby. Continental breakfast is
included. Facilities include eco
tours, fishing and golf.

Stephanie's Hotel $$
Rodney Bay
☎ 450-8689
20 comfortable rooms plus the
lively Crab Hole Restaurant and
Party Place.

St James Club $$$
Morgan Bay
☎ 450-2511
All inclusive, 238 room beach
resort with restaurants, pool,
watersports and tennis.

Still Plantation and
Beach Resort $$
PO Box 246, Soufrière
☎ 459-7224
Set in lush, tropical gardens, the
resort offers the chance to experience life on a real tropical plantation. There are 13 self-contained
apartments and studios, and
beachfront accommodation.
Facilities include an excellent
restaurant serving island specialities, bars, beach, laundry service
and pool.

Ti Kaye Village $$-$$$
Anse Cochon, between Anse
La Raye and Canaries
☎ 758-456-8101
This is a gem, truly the place to get
away from it all. It is truly the place
to get away from it all. Nestled
along a cliff on the west coast, the
"village" has 33 traditional West
Indian-style cottages around the
main pavilion housing the Kai
Manje restaurant (House of Food),
bar and pool and fabulous pano-
ramic views of the caribbean. each

cottage is sited to afford privacy
and to catch the breezes. Facilities
include scuba, snorkeling and other
water sports, fitness center,
massage and tours are organized.

Tropical Haven Mini Hotel $
PO Box 615, Castries
☎ 452-3505
On the La Toc coastline overlooking
Castries, with ten comfortable
rooms and private patios. Downtown Castries, shopping and the
nearest beach are all within walking
distance. Facilities include restaurant, bar and sundeck.

Villa Beach Cottages $
Choc Beach
PO Box 129, Castries
☎ 450-2884
Five lovely cottages set in tropical
gardens, a few yards from the
beach. Facilities include restaurant
and bar, maid service, laundry
service, babysitting, supermarket
with neary shopping.

Windjammer Landing Villa
Beach Resort $$-$$$
Labrellotte Bay
PO Box 1504, Castries
☎ 456-9000,
US 800-743-9609,
Canada 800-267-7600,
UK 800-373-742
Luxury fully-equipped 232 rooms
and villas with private plunge pools
suitable for families and honey-
mooners alike. Facilities include 3
restaurants, bars, pools and kiddie
pools, supervised children's
activities, tennis, watersports, car
rental, health and beauty centre.

GUESTHOUSES

Alexander's Guest House
Gros Islet, 8 rooms
☎ 450-8610

Alizee Inn
Gros Islet, 8 rooms
☎ 452-0960

Bay Mini Guesthouse
Gros Islet, 4 rooms
☎ 450-8956

Beach Walk Inn
Choc Bay, 4 rooms
☎ 451-7888

Blue Lagoon
Castries, 21 rooms
☎ 450-8453

Bon Appetit Inn
Castries, 5 rooms
☎ 452-2757

Chateau Blanc Guest House $
Morne-Du-Don Road,
Chaussee, Castries
☎ 452-1851
Friendly, family run 7 room guest-house 5 minutes from downtown Castries. It is 15 minutes to the beach. Breakfast and dinner are served on request.

Chez Camilla's Guest House
Soufriere
☎ 459-5440

Country Cottage Motel
Reduit Park
☎ 458-0052

Dornelly's Inn
Castries, 12 2-bedroom
apartments
☎ 452-5561

Daphil's Mini Hotel
Gros Islet, 10 rooms
☎ 450-9318

Hillside Plaza
Castries, 30 rooms
☎ 452-4371

La Panache Guest House
Gros Islet, 5 rooms
☎ 450-0765

Manje Domi
Desruisseaux, 4 rooms with
restaurant
☎ 455-0729

Modern Inn
Castries, 8 rooms
☎ 452-4001

Parrot's Hideaway
Castries, 7 rooms
☎ 452-0726

St Martin's Guesthoue
Vieux Fort, 7 rooms
☎ 454-6674

VILLAS AND APARTMENTS

Nelson's Furnished Apartments
Castries
☎ 450-8275

Seaview Apartment
Castries
☎ 452-2469

Seagrape Apartments
Rodney Bay
☎ 452-8358

Stonefield Estate Villas $$$
☎ 459-7037
Set in 26 acres just south of Soufriere, with 11 elegant villas, restaurant, pools and magnificent views.

Fact File

Sweet Shaves Apartments
The Morne
☎ 452-2311

Top of the Morne Apartments
Morn Fortune
☎ 452-3603

Tropical Breeze
Gros Islet
☎ 450-0589

Tropical Villas
Castries
☎ 450-8240

Tuxedo Villas
Reduit
☎ 452-8553

Villa Apartments
The Morne
☎ 452-2691

Villa Beach Cottages
Castries
☎ 450-2884

Villa Zandoli
Rodney Bay
☎ 452-8898

AIRLINES

Air Canada
Castries ☎ 452-2550,
Hewanorra ☎ 454-6038

Air Jamaica
☎ 453-6611

Air France
Castries ☎ 458-8282

American Airlines
George Charles Airport
☎ 454-6777, Micoud Street,
Hewanorra ☎ 454-6777

BWIA International
Brazil Street, Castries
☎ 800-538-2942,
Hewanorra ☎ 454-5075
In the US ☎ 1-800-JET-BWIA

British Airways
☎ 452-3951/7444

Eastern Caribbean Helicopters
☎ 453-6952

LIAT
☎ 452-5856

St Lucia Helicopters
Pointe Seraphine
☎ 453-6950

US Airways
☎ 800-622-1015

Virgin Atlantic
☎ 454-3610/800-744-7477

BANKS

Banks are open Monday to Friday 8am-3pm, and until 5pm on Fridays. Banks are generally closed at weekends and on public holidays, although Barclays, National Commercial Bank and the Royal Bank of Canada have Saturday morning hours.

Bank of Nova Scotia
William Peter Blvd, Castries
☎ 456-2100

Bank of St Lucia
Soufrière
☎ 456-6000

Caribbean Banking Corporation
Gablewoods Shopping Mall
☎ 451-7469/453-2265

First Caribbean International Bank
Bridge Street, Castries
Castries ☎ 456-100
Soufriere ☎ 459-7255
Rodney Bay Marina ☎ 452-9384

Royal Bank of Canada
William Peter Boulevard and Laborie Street in Castries and Rodney Bay Marina
☎ 456-9200

St Lucia Co-operative Bank
Bridge Street, Castries
☎ 455-7000 and Rodney Bay
☎ 452-8882

BEAUTY SALONS AND HAIRDRESSERS

Many of the resorts have their own facilities. Others include:
Betty May's Hair Design Chisel and St Louis Streets, Castries
☎ 453-2864

Classix Hair Design
Rex St. Lucian
☎ 452-0264

Heads Up
Chaussee, Castries
☎ 453-6515

Health and Beauty Day Spa
Bois d'Orange ☎ 452-8031
Mag's Unisex Hair Shop
Casa St Lucia, Vigie
☎ 452-4096

Salon Lesport
Castries
☎ 457-7867

Strandz Hair and Nail Studio
Gablewoods Mall
☎ 451-3304

Suzie's Beauty Salon
Brazil Street, Castries
☎ 452-1680

▲ **Fact File**

125

Fact File

BOOKSHOPS

Sunshine Bookshop
Gablewoods and J.Q's Mall
☎ 452-3222

Book Salon
Jeremie and Laborie St, Castries
☎ 452-3817

BICYCLES

St Lucia Mountain Bike Tour ☎ 452-4049

BUSINESS HOURS

Commercial: Monday-Friday 8am-12noon, 1.30-4pm,
                Saturday 8.30am-12.30pm.
Government: Monday-Friday 8am-12.30pm and 1.30-4.30pm.

CAMPING

The main campsite is at Anse La Liberté, south of Canaries. It can be reached by water taxi from Canaries or by foot along a descending trail from Belvederc ☎ 452-5005. There is a smaller campsite at Fond d'or Dennery ☎ 453-3242.

CAR RENTAL

Cars and 4 wheel drive vehicles can be rented and provide the best way of exploring the island. If you plan to go at peak periods, it is best to rent your vehicle in advance through your travel agent. Cars can be rented at airports, hotels or car rental offices on the island.

Rental car rates range from US$ 300 to 400 a week depending on the type of vehicle and the rental company. Average daily rates are around US$65 and this does not include insurance which costs an additional US$15-20 a day.

A temporary St Lucia driving licence is required, and can be obtained on production of your current driving licence on arrival at the airport, the police station in Castries or the car rental office. It costs EC$54 (US $21).

RULES OF THE ROAD

DRIVE ON THE LEFT. The roads are generally good and there is a substantial road improvement programme under way. In rural areas, however, you have to be on the look out for potholes, fallen branches, and coconuts in the roads and so on. Don't speed because you never know what may be round the next corner. The St Lucians' love of cricket encourages them to play at every opportunity, and the road makes an ideal pitch!

Seat belts should be worn at all times. The speed limit is 30mph (48kph) in Castries, and there is no reason to go very much faster out of town because you will not fully appreciate the scenery.

Drinking and driving is against the law, and there are heavy penalties if convicted, especially if it resulted in an accident.

Avoid clearly marked 'no parking' zones or you might pick up a ticket, but parking generally does not pose a problem, even in Castries.

If you have an accident or breakdown during the day, call your car rental company so make sure you have the telephone number with you. They will usually send out a mechanic or a replacement vehicle. If you are stuck at night make sure the car is off the road, lock the vehicle and call a taxi to take you back to your hotel. Report the problem to the car rental company or the police as soon as possible. Remember to drive in St Lucia you should be a PHD – Pot Hole Dodger!

Rental companies

Avis Rent a Car	☎ 451-6976 / ☎ 452-2700
Ben's West coast Jeep	☎ 459-5457
Budget Rent a Car	☎ 452-8673
CC Rentals	☎ 459-5771 / ☎ 451-9452
Cool Breeze Jeep Car Rental	☎ 459-7729 / ☎ 454-7898
Cost Less Rent a Car	☎ 450-3416
Courtesy Car Rentals	☎ 452-8140
Courtesy Rent a Car	☎ 452-8140
Hertz	☎ 454-9636 / ☎ 452-0680
National Car Rental	☎ 450-8721
St Lucia Yacht Club Rental	☎ 452-5057
Wayne's Motorcycle Centre	☎ 452-2059

Fact File

CHURCHES

Nearly 90 per cent of St Lucian's are Catholic, but many other denominations are represented on the island, including Anglican, Methodist, Baptist, Seventh Day Adventist, Church of the Nazarene, Christian Science and the Salvation Army. Times of services vary at individual churches so inquire at your hotel reception.

CURRENCY

The official currency on the island is the East Caribbean dollar although US dollars are accepted almost everywhere. EC$ come in the following denominations: 5, 10, 20, 50 and 100 with 1c, 2c, 5c, 10c, 25c 50c and one dollar coins.

The banks offer a fixed, and generally a better rate of exchange than hotels and shops. Traveller's cheques, preferably in US dollars, are also accepted in hotels and large stores, and all major credit cards can be used in hotels, large stores and restaurants. There are several ATM machines around the island.

Note: Always make certain that you know what currency you are dealing in when arranging a taxi ride, guide, charter and so on. First establish the currency (either EC$ or US$) and then agree a price. It could save a lot of arguments later on.

Note: Always have a few small denomination notes, either US$1 or EC$5 notes for tips.

DEPARTURE TAX

There is a departure tax of EC$54 (US$21) for all passengers leaving the island (and a security tax of US $4 for LIAT passengers). If departing from Vigie airport, buy some food and drink before you go through to the departure lounge as there are limited facilities.

DISABLED FACILITIES

There are facilities for the disabled at most of the larger resorts, but not much elsewhere.

DRESS CODE

Casual is the keyword but you can be as smart or as cool as you like. Beachwear is fine for the beach and pool areas, but cover up a little for the street. Wear a hat if planning to be out in the sun for a long time. Dressing up for dinner can be fun.

Fact File

ELECTRICITY

The usual electricity supply is 220 volts, 50 cycles alternating current, and most sockets take UK-style 3 pin plugs. Some hotels, however, also have 110 volt supplies which are suitable for US appliances. Adapters are generally available at the hotels, or can be purchased if you do not travel with your own.

EMBASSIES AND CONSULATES

British High Commission
N.I.S Building, Waterfront,
2nd floor, Castries
☎ 452-2484
(Monday to Friday
8.30am-12.30pm)

**Embassy of the
Republic of China**
Cap Estate
☎ 450-8300
(Monday to Friday
8am-12noon and 2-4pm)

**Federal Republic of Germany
Consulate**
PO Box 2025, Gros Inlet
☎ 450-8050
(Monday to Friday 8am-
12.30pm and 1.30-4.30 pm)

French Embassy
Vigie, Castries
☎ 455-6060
(Open Monday, Tuesday,
Thursday & Friday 8am-3pm.
Wednesdays 1-5pm)

Italian Consulate
Reduit, PO Box GM 848
☎ 452-0866
(Monday to Friday 1-4pm)

Netherlands Consulate
M&C Building,
Bridge Street,
PO Box 1020,
Castries
☎ 452-3592
(Monday to Friday
8am-4.30pm)

**Organisation of American
States**
Vigie, Castries
☎ 452-4330
(Monday to Friday 8.30am-
12.30pm and 1.30- 4.30pm)

Venezuelan Embassy
Casa Vigie, Castries
☎ 452-4033

EMERGENCY TELEPHONE NUMBERS

For Police, Fire and Ambulance   ☎ 911

Air and Sea Rescue   ☎ 452-2894/452

Tourist Board   ☎ 452-5968/452-4094

Fact File

ESSENTIAL THINGS TO PACK

Sun tan cream, sunglasses, sun hat, camera (and lots of film), insect repellent, binoculars (if interested in bird watching and wildlife) and a small torch in case of power failures.

FESTIVALS/CALENDAR OF EVENTS

January 1	New Years Day
February 22	Independence Day
April	Holy Week – April Festival of Comedy
May	International Jazz Festival
June/July	Fisherman's Feast (Fet peche). Carnival, a two day extravaganza just prior to Lent
August	Rose Festival – Market Festival
October	International Creole Day. St Lucia BH Fishing Tournament
November 22	St Cecilia's Day. Island musicians celebrate the patron saint of music
December 13	St Lucia's Day, National Day. Christmas Folk Fiesta

FISHING

Fishing is an island pursuit, and many St Lucians will fish for hours from harbour walls, from the beach or riverside. Deep sea and game fishing is mostly for blue marlin and tuna which can weigh up to 1,000lbs (450kgm) wahoo and white marlin, which can weigh more than 100lbs (45kgm) and the fighting sailfish. Snapper, grouper, bonito, dorado and barracuda can all be kept close to shore. There are a number of boats available for charter or which offer deep sea fishing:

Boating in Paradise
Bois D'Orange
☎ 458-0170

Captain Bravo
☎ 451-4064

Captain Mike's Watersports
Vigie Marina
☎ 452-7044

Endless Summers
☎ 450-8651

Hackshaws Boat Charter & Sports Fishing
☎ 453-0553

Mako Watersports
Rodney Bay Marina
☎ 452-0412

The Moorings
☎ 451-4357

HEALTH

There are no serious health problems although visitors should take precautions against the sun and mosquitoes, both of which can ruin your holiday. Immunisation is not required unless travelling from an infected area within six days of arrival.

All hotels have doctors either resident or on call. A resident doctor's visit normally costs between EC$40-50 (US$16-20).

HOSPITALS

There are four hospitals on the island:

Golden Hope ☎ 452-2289	**Soufrière** ☎ 459-7258
Gros Islet ☎ 450-9661	**Tapion** ☎ 459-2000
Victoria Hospital ☎ 452-2421	**Dennery** ☎ 453-3310
St Jude's Vieux Fort ☎ 454-6041	

HURRICANES

St Lucia is fortunate in that it has suffered less from hurricanes than most other Caribbean islands, although Hurricane Allen did devastating damage when it came ashore in 1980. The hurricane season for St Lucia is between August and early October, with September the most likely month for tropical storms, although almost all of these pass by safely north of the island.

INOCULATIONS

Inoculations are only required for visitors travelling from infected areas.

IRRITATING INSECTS

Mosquitoes can be a problem almost anywhere. In your room, burn mosquito coils or use one of the many electrical plug-in devices which burn an insect repelling tablet. Mosquitoes are not so much of a problem on or near the beaches because of onshore winds, but they may well bite you as you enjoy an open air evening meal. Use a good insect repellent, particularly if you are planning trips inland such as walking in the rain forests.

Lemon grass can be found growing naturally, and a handful of this in your room is a useful mosquito deterrent.

Sand flies can be a problem on the beach. Despite their tiny size they can give you a nasty bite. Ants abound, so make sure you check the ground carefully before sitting down otherwise you might get bitten, and the bites can itch for days. There are several creams available to relieve itchiness from bites and Bay Rum Cologne is also a good remedy when dabbed on the skin.

LANGUAGE

The official language spoken is English, although most people speak a French-based Patois.

LOST PROPERTY

Report lost property as soon as possible to your hotel or the nearest police station.

MUSIC

Music is a way of life and the philosophy is the louder it is played, the better. Cars, mini-van buses and open doorways all seem to blast out music, and once the music starts it goes on for hours. When the St Lucia's party, it often lasts all night, and the Friday night 'jump up' in Gros Islet attracts thousands each week.

St Lucia is also known for its week-long international jazz festival held each May, which attracts world class performers in a variety of venues, from intimate clubs to spectacular open air settings under the stars on Pigeon Island.

NATURE TOURS & TRAILS

WORTH VISITING

Barre de L'Isle Trail — A trek along the ridge that divides the eastern and western parts of the island and a climb to the summit of Mt La Combe.

Des Castries Rainforest — Explore St Lucia's most hidden rainforest. An all day tour. ☎ 450-2231

Diamond Falls — Diamond Estate

Eastern Nature Trail — 3.5 miles (5.6Km) along the east coast from Mandele to Praslin Bay. ☎ 453-7656

Fact
File

Grande Anse Beach — Turtle watching mid-March to end of July. Watches held on Saturday nights between 4pm-6am. Contact ☎ 452-8100. There is a small charge.

Latille Gardens — Waterfalls and wildlife ☎ 454-0202

Mankote Mangrove — Vast swamp area rich in bird and marine life.

Mt Gimie — Great views and rich flora/fauna

Sulphur Springs — Soufrière

NATURE HIKES/TRAILS

Barre de L'isle Rain Forest Trail — To the summit of Morne La Combe, 3 hours.

Edmund Forest Reserve — Strenuous but beautiful $3\frac{1}{2}$ hour nature walk.

Enbas Saut Falls Trail — Starts 6 miles east of soufière and runs for 4km to twin falls. remote and beautiful.

Union Nature Trail — One hour, information centre.

Fregate Island — Tours arranged by St Lucia.

Nature Trail — National Trust.

Morne Le Blanc — Trail Laborie.

Hardy Point Cactus Valley Walking Trek — Starts at Hardy Point.

PERSONAL INSURANCE AND MEDICAL COVER

Make sure you have adequate personal insurance and medical cover. If you need to call out a doctor or have medical treatment, you will probably have to pay for it at the time, so keep all receipts so that you can reclaim on your insurance.

PHARMACIES

There are a number of pharmacies in Castries – Clarke's and Williams are both in Bridge Street, M&C's is in Bridge Street, Gablewoods, J.Q's Mall, Rodney Bay & J.Q's Plaza, Vieux Fort. Marcellin's is on the corner of Micoud and Chisel Streets, Marshall's is on the corner of Brazil and Broglie Streets and Regis Pharmacy is on the Morne du Don road. The St Lucia Health and

Utility Services Clinic (with doctor and pharmacy) is on the Gros
Islet Highway. Most hotels have 'over the counter' medication.

PHOTOGRAPHY

The intensity of the sun can play havoc with your films, especially if
photographing near water or white sand. Compensate for the
brightness otherwise your photographs will come out over-ex-
posed. The heat can actually damage film so store reels in a box or
bag in the hotel fridge if there is one. Also remember to protect
your camera if on the beach, as a single grain of sand is all it takes
to jam your camera.

It is very easy to get 'click happy' in the Caribbean, but be tactful
when taking photographs. Many islanders are shy or simply fed up
with being photographed, and others will insist on a small pay-
ment. You will have to decide whether the photograph is worth it,
but if a person declines to have their photograph taken, do not
ignore this. St Lucian's are a warm and very hospitable race and if
you stop and spend some time finding out what they are doing,
they will usually then allow you to take a photograph.

POLICE

Police Headquarters is in Bridge Street, Castries. ☎ 452 3854/5

PORTS

The main port is Castries and there are also deep water facilities for
cargo and container ships at Vieux Fort in the south near the
international airport. There are also many marinas.

POST OFFICES

Post Office hours are 8.30am-4.30pm Monday to Friday and
Saturday 8am-12noon. There are post offices in most towns.

PUBLIC TOILETS

There are not many public toilets on the island, but bars, restaurants and hotels have private facilities, which can usually be used if
you ask politely.

RESTAURANTS

There is a remarkably large choice when it comes to eating out on
the island. There are the inevitable fast food burger, pizza and fried
chicken outlets, beach cafes offering excellent value for money and

Fact File

elegant upmarket dining rooms, as well as restaurants offering a wide range of ethnic cuisines, from Creole and Caribbean cooking to Chinese.

Most accept credit cards and during peak times of the year, reservations are recommended.

The restaurants listed in the itineraries are classified by price ($ inexpensive, $$ moderate, $$$ expensive), by our own star system (from one to four) which is based on quality of food, service and ambience.

SEA TRIPS

(See also Yacht Charter under Sport page)

Brig Unicorn (used in the TV drama Roots), the ship is also used in "Pirates of the Caribbean", sails from Vigie Cove on Monday and Friday morning for Soufrière and area visit. Includes buffet lunch, rum punch, snorkelling, swimming and visit to Marigot Bay. Arrives back around 4.30pm. ☎ 452-8644

Captain Yannis, day and half day cruises from Union Island. Fly from St Lucia to board. Available through local travel agents.

Endless Summer 1 and 11, 56ft (17m) catamarans offering full day sail tours to Soufrière and area, snorkelling plus sunset cruises. ☎ 450-8651

Hackshaws Boat Charters, ☎ 453-0553

Mango Tango Catamaran, ☎ 452-8644 or ☎ 458-0123.

Mystic Man Tours, ☎ 459-7783. Fleet of vessels for yacht charters, snorkeling, sunset cruises and airport transfers.

SECURITY

St Lucia has a low crime rate but it makes sense like anywhere else, not to walk around wearing expensive jewellery or flashing large sums of money. Do not carry your passport around, traveller's cheques or all your money. Keep them secure in your room or in a hotel safety deposit box. It is also a good idea to have photocopies of the information page of your passport, your air ticket and holiday insurance policy. All will help greatly if the originals are lost.

As with most tourist destinations, you might be pestered by touts trying to sell tours, souvenirs and even drugs, or by young people begging. A firm 'no' or 'not interested', is normally enough to persuade them to try someone else.

Do not be alarmed at the large numbers of people who walk around with machetes. These are used throughout the island as a gardening implement.

SERVICE CHARGES AND TAXES

There is a Government tax of 8 per cent on all hotel and restaurant bills, and a service charge of 10 per cent is usually added. Menus and tariffs sometimes include these charges so check to make sure they have not been added again. In shops, the price on the label is what you pay. When buying in markets and from street vendors, try haggling over the price.

SIGHTSEEING

Sightseeing and island tours by land or sea can be organised through hotels, tour representatives or one of the many specialist tour companies on the island. These include:

ATV Adventures	☎ 458-8282/3/4
Barefoot Holidays	☎ 450-0507
Barnards Travel	☎ 452-2214
Fletchers Touring Agency	☎ 452-2516
Heritage Tours	☎ 458-1726/451-6058
Island Adventures Co	☎ 450-4491
Island Bike Hikes	☎ 458-0908
Jungle Bike Adventure	☎ 451-2453
Sailaway Tours	☎ 452-9842
Solar Tours	☎ 452-5898
Spice Travel	☎ 452-0866
St Lucia Helicopters	☎ 453-6952
Sunlink/St Lucia Reps	☎ 456-9100

SPORT

Cricket is the national game and played with such a fervour that it is not surprising that the West Indies are world champions. The game is played at every opportunity and anywhere. You can be driving in the countryside, turn a corner and confront players using the road as a wicket. It is played on the beach and even in the water if the tide is coming in. If the island team or the West Indies is playing, almost all the radios on the island are tuned in for the commentary. When cricket is not being played, football is the top sport.

For the visitor, there is a huge range of sporting opportunities from swimming, scuba diving, horseback riding, hiking, golf, tennis, cycling, sailing, squash and, of course, fishing either from shore or boat. The Atlantic coastline offers stronger swell for windsurfing and surfing but the seas can sometimes be very rough and care is needed, while the Caribbean beaches offer safe swimming. Swimming in slow moving rivers and lakes is not advisable because of the risk of bilharzia, a disease caused by a parasitic water-borne worm.

Most hotels offer a variety of sports and water activities, and there are diving schools where you can learn what it is all about and progress to advanced level if you have the time. There is even organised jogging! Roadbusters meet outside J.Q. Charles's Supermarket at La Clery on Tuesday, Wednesday and Thursday afternoons at 5pm.

Walking is great fun and there are lots of trails, especially in the mountains but have stout, non-slip footwear and a waterproof. Protect yourself against insects, carry adequate drinking water and keep an eye on the time, because night falls quickly and you don't want to be caught out on the trail after dark. Guides can be arranged to escort you on these walks and make sure you get the most out of your trip.

FACILITIES

Cycling

Jungle Biking
Anse Chastanet
☎ 451-BIKE

Fitness Gyms/Exercise Centres

Body Inc
Gablewoods Mall
☎ 451-9744

La Borde's Gym
Old La Toc Road, Castries
☎ 452-2788

Mango Moon Total Fitness
Vigie Cove
☎ 453-1934

St Lucia Racquet Club
Club St Lucia, Cap Estate
☎ 450-0551

Sportivo and Jazzercise
Above the Key Largo Restaurant,
Rodney Heights ☎ 452-8899

Golf

Jalousie Hilton Resort
Executive Par 3 course & Spa
☎ 459-7666

St Lucia Golf & Country Club Estate
Cap Estate ☎ 450-8523

Sandals La Toc
☎ 452-3081

Horseback Riding

Country Saddles
☎ 450-0197

International Pony Club
Beauséjour, Gros Islet
☎ 452-8139

Trim's Riding Stables
Cas-en-Bas ☎ 452-8273

Tennis

Almost all the resorts and many of the hotels have their own tennis courts, often floodlit.

Squash

St Lucia Yacht Club
Reduit Beach ☎ 452-8491/8350

St Lucia Racquet Club
Club St Lucia, Cap Estate
☎ 450-0551

Fact File

Scuba

St Lucia is ideal for divers, from beginners to the most experienced. The waters are warm, visibility is excellent and the reef abounds with an amazing variety of marine and plant life. You can swim among the nurse sharks, turtles and shoals of tropical fish which live around the many artificial reefs that have grown up around the many sunken ships. There is a wide variety of fragile coral, from huge gorgonians, black lace, barrel and purple vase sponges.

Some of the more spectacular dive sites include Key Hole Pinnacles, four columns which rise from the depths to their summit just below the surface, and Superman's Flight, a drift dive along a wall that drops to 1,600 feet (488m) that is just off Petit Piton. Just up the coast, off Gros Piton, are the Coral Gardens, five fingers of coral that vary in depth from 15 to 50 feet (4.5 to 15m). There is also a spectacular wall and drift dive off Anse La Raye, while off the point of Anse Chastanet, the reefs gradually fall away to a depth of 140 feet (42.5m).

The best wreck drives are the Waiwinette, a freighter which lies in 90 feet (27.5m) of water to the south of the island, and the Volga, which lies in 20 feet (6m) of water off Castries. The first dive is for experienced divers only because of the strong currents, while the Volga is suitable for all qualified divers.

The newest reef is developing around the Lesleen M that was sunk by the St. Lucia Department of Fisheries in 1985 in 60 (18m) feet of water near Anse Cochon on the west coast south of Marigot Bay.

Buddies
Rodney Bay Marina
☎ 450-8406

Caribbean Dive Center
Harmony Suites
☎ 452-9910

Dolphin Divers
Anse Chastanet
☎ 452-9485

Marigot Beach Club & Dive Resort
Marigot Bay
☎ 451-4974

SCUBA St Lucia
Anse Chastanet and Rex St Lucian ☎ 459-7755

Undersea Adventures
Vigie Cove, Castries
☎ 450-1640

Dive Fair Helen
☎ 450-1640

Frog's Driving Ltd
Harmony Suites, Rodney Bay
☎ 458-0798

Water Sports

Available at all resorts and most large hotels.

Parasailing St Lucia is based at the Rex St Lucian ☎ 452-8351;

The best windsurfing spots are: The east coast offers the best windsurfing for those with experience while the calmer west coast is ideal for beginners. Most beachside hotels and resorts offer instructors and equipment although the most popular locations are Cas-en-bas and Vieux Fort.

Fact File

Yacht Charter and Private Moorings

There is a huge range of vessels and crews for charter for sailing, sightseeing, fishing and diving. Marigot Bay and Rodney Bay, both on the north-eastern coast, are the two most popular marinas.

Companies offering yacht charters are:

Brig Unicorn
☎ 452-8644 or ☎ 458-0123

Cats Inc
☎ 450-8651

Destination St Lucia
☎ 452-8531

DSL Yachting
Rodney Bay Marina
☎ 452-8531

Endless Summer
☎ 450-8651

Francis Sailing Tours
☎ 459-54433

Moorings St Lucia
☎ 452-4256

Sea Spray Cruises Ltd
☎ 452-8644

Stevens Yachts
☎ 452-8648

STAMPS

The St Lucia Philatelic Bureau, at the General Post Office, in Bridge Street, Castries (☎ 452-3774) offers the island's commemorative stamps for sale – and they are excellent. Commemorative sets are issued every year, and whether you are interested in stamp collecting or not, they make wonderful mementoes, as they feature St Lucian history, wildlife, celebrities and special occasions.

The island's first stamps were issued on 18 December 1860, and the island's first airmail letters were sent on 22 September 1929, aboard a Pan American Airways flight piloted by Captain Charles Lindbergh.

TAXIS

Courtesy
☎ 452-3555

City Taxi Service
☎ 452-3154

North Lime Taxi Assoc
☎ 452-8562

Southern Tax Assoc
☎ 454-6136

Vigie Airport Taxi Assoc
☎ 452-1599

TELEPHONES

If you wondered where Britain's red telephone boxes went, the answer is that many ended up in St Lucia. There are lots of public telephones on the island. They are operated by Cable and Wireless

Fact File

and most accept coins and phone cards. Phone cards can be purchased at many locations including hotels, shops, airports, marinas and tourist offices. The phone cards can also be used on most of the English-speaking Windward Islands.

Faxes can be sent from most hotels and through the Cable & Wireless office in Castries, and if you have any communications problems, visit their offices where you will find them most helpful.

The international dialling code for St Lucia is 1 758. From the United States, dialling St Lucia is a long distance call, dial 1 758 and the seven digit number. From the United Kingdom 00 1 758 and then the seven digit St Lucia number.

For credit card calls from St Lucia dial 811, or 1-800-877-8000. For USA Direct dial 1-800-872-2881, for Call USA dial 1-800-674-7000, for Sprint Express dial 1-800-277-7468, for BT Direct Service, dial 1-800-342-5284 and for Canada Direct dial 1-800-744-2580.

TIME

St Lucia is four hours behind Greenwich Mean Time and one hour ahead of Eastern Time in the United States. If it is noon in London it is 8am in St Lucia, and when it is noon in New York, it is 1pm on the island.

While it is important to know the time so that you do not miss your flight, time becomes less important the longer you stay on the island. If you order a taxi it will generally be early or arrive on time, and if you have a business meeting it will start on schedule, for almost everything else be prepared to adopt 'Caribbean time', especially in bars, restaurants and shops. Don't confuse this relaxed attitude with laziness or rudeness, it is just the way things are done in the islands, and the quicker you accept this, the sooner you will start to relax and enjoy yourselves.

TIPPING

Tips are not generally added to bills but it is customary to tip bell hops in hotels, taxi drivers, guides and other people providing a service. Tip taxi drivers around 10-12 per cent and bell hops EC$1-2 for each piece of luggage.

TOURIST INFORMATION

The St Lucia Tourist Board is based at Pointe Seraphine and is open from 8am-4.30pm Monday to Saturday. If a cruise ship is in port on Sunday or a public holiday, the office opens for half a day.

There is also an information office in Soufrière, open 8.30am-4pm Monday to Friday, and 8.30am-12.30pm on Saturday. There are also information centres at Jeremie Street in Castries and at both Vigie (☎ 452-4094) and Hewanorra airports (☎ 454-6644).

Hotels also provide information through their front desks.

Canada	8 King St. East suite 700 Toronto, Ontario M5c 1B5 ☎ 416-362-4242, Fax: 416-362-7832	**France**	A.N.I. 53 Rue Francois Ler, 75008 Paris ☎ 47-20-39-66, Fax: 47-23-09-65
St Lucia	Pointe Seraphine, PO Box 221, Castries ☎ 758-452-5968/4094, Fax: 758-453-1121	**Germany**	Postfach 1525, 61366 Friedrichsdorf ☎ 49-6172-778013, Fax: 49-6172-778033
UK	St Lucia Tourist Board, 421a Finchley Rd, London NW3 6HJ ☎ 0207-431-3675, Fax: 0207-431-7920	**USA**	820 2nd Avenue, 9th floor New York NY 10017, USA ☎ 212-867-2950 Fax: 212-867-2795

TOUR OPERATORS

There are many tour operators on the island and all offer a number of trips and excursions, or can tailor make itinerares to suit you. Many of the tours sound the same, so check to see that you are getting value for money, or getting something special. Main operators are on the next page.

Barefoot Holidays
(St Lucia) Rodney Bay
Industrial Estate
☎ 450-0507

Barnard's Travel
Micoud and Bridge Street,
Castries
☎ 452-2214

Carib Travel
Micoud Street, Castries
☎ 452-3176, and Clarke Street,
Vieux Fort ☎ 452-2151

**Conference and
Incentive Services**
☎ 252-7058

Hibiscus Travel Soufrière
☎ 459-5218, and Bourbon
Street, Castries
☎ 453-1527

**International Travel
Consultants**
Bourbon House, Bourbon Street,
Castries
☎ 452-3131

M&C Tourist Department
Bridge Street, Castries
☎ 458-8281

Pitons Travel Agency
Richard Fanis Building
Marisule
☎ 450-1486/7

St Lucia Helicopters
Pointe Seraphine
☎ 453-6952

St Lucia Reps/Sunlink Tours
Reduit Beach Avenue
☎ 456-9100

Solar Tours & Travel
Bridge Street, Castries
☎ 452-5898

Fact File

Spice Travel
Reduit Park, Rodney Bay
☎ 452-0866

Sun Fun Tours
☎ 452-5233

Sunlink International
Reduit ☎ 452-8929
and Club St Lucia by Splash
☎ 456-9199

Travel World
John Compton Highway, Castries
☎ 451-7443

VISA

Visitors from the US and Commonwealth Countries need to present a valid passport, ID or birth certificate, plus onward ticket. Visitors from other countries require a passport and visa.

WATER

It is advisable to boil tap water for drinking. Bottled mineral and distilled water is widely available.

WEDDINGS

St Lucia is a popular destination for honeymoon couples, and lots of other couples get carried away by the romance of the island and decide to marry while on vacation. If you decide to marry, you must file an application to be married after you have been resident on the island for two days. This application can be made through a local solicitor to the Attorney General. Many hotels also offer wedding packages and will make all the arrangements for you. The application must be filed at least two working days before the date of the wedding. Most denominations of church weddings can be arranged in advance, and registrars usually charge a fee plus travel costs. Valentines Day is a very popular day for weddings, and registrars are usually very busy rushing around conducting marriage after marriage.

Fees: Norarial fees & marriage licence EC $302-50, Registrar fees EC $120, Marriage certificate EC $8.

YOUTH HOSTELS

Limited youth hostel-style accommodation is available through the National Research Development Foundation in Castries (☎ 452-4253). It has about 8 multi-bedded rooms to accommodate students, and can also recommend a number of small guest houses offering friendly, budget accommodation.